Praise for Fierce

Jen highlights lesser-known but highly courageous women with character and guts enough to enter into Kingdom-building conversations and actions. She challenges us to explore not only the biblical narrative but our own stories as well so that we can influence our world as our spiritual sisters in the faith influenced theirs. A worthy study.

—**Carolyn Moore**, Founding and Lead Pastor of Mosaic United Methodist Church in Evans, Georgia, and author of *The 19: Questions to Kindle a Wesleyan Spirit*

If you dream of blazing trails in Jesus' name, this study provides the biblical backbone to strengthen your faith and build Christ-confidence along the way. I love Jen's boldness in calling women to God-honoring discipleship as well as her authenticity in sharing the highs and lows in her own journey. I highly recommend it!

—**Barb Roose**, speaker and author of *I'm Waiting, God: Finding Blessing in God's Delays, Joshua: Winning the Worry Battle*, and other Bible studies and books

The bold message behind Jen Cowart's new study, *Fierce*, is that the faithfulness of ordinary women can change the world. This study is a much-needed and beautifully written breath of fresh air for women who want to know that our lives matter. The deep biblical truths in this study are a welcome and enriching guide for those who long to live fierce lives for Jesus.

—**Jessica LaGrone**, Dean of Chapel, Asbury Seminary

Once again Jennifer boldly yet gently leads women to wrestle with Scripture and real life. Using stories of strong, vibrant women of the Bible, she has created a "space" for the Holy Spirit to shape the life and character of women.

—**Jorge Acevedo**, Lead Pastor, Grace Church, a multisite United Methodist Congregation

Jim and Jennifer Cowart are highly respected pastors and church leaders who lead model purpose-driven churches. I have full confidence in Jim and Jen.

—**Rick Warren**, Founder and Senior Pastor of Saddleback Church and author of *The Purpose Driven Life* and numerous other books

FIERCE

Women of the Bible Who Changed the World

A BIBLE STUDY BY

Jennifer Cowart

Abingdon Women/Nashville

Fierce
Women of the Bible Who Changed the World

ISBN 978-1-5018-8290-6

20 21 22 23 24 25 26 27 28 — 10 9 8 7 6 5 4 3 2
MANUFACTURED IN THE UNITED STATES OF AMERICA

To my mom, Linda, and my daughter, Alyssa—
two of the fiercest women I have ever known

About the Author

Jennifer Cowart is the executive pastor at Harvest Church, a United Methodist congregation in Warner Robins, Georgia, that she and her husband, Jim, began in 2001. With degrees in Christian education, counseling, and business, she has been integral to the development of the Emerging and Discipleship Ministries at Harvest, including more than three hundred small groups that meet in homes and workplaces. As a gifted Bible teacher and speaker, Jen brings biblical truth to life through humor, authenticity, and everyday application. She is the author of the Bible study *Messy People: Life Lessons from Imperfect Biblical Heroes* and coauthor with her husband, Jim, of several small group studies, including *Hand Me Downs* and *Living the Five*. They are the proud parents of two children, Alyssa and Joshua, and have a son-in-law, Andrew.

Follow Jen:

Website: jennifercowart.org or jimandjennifercowart.org
           (check here for event dates and booking information)

Jim-Jennifer Cowart

jimandjennifercowart

Contents

Introduction

The word *fierce* is trendy. It's used to describe women who are extreme athletes, high-level executives, and supermodels. It describes women who are at the top of their game and making a difference in the world. In fact, if you look up the word *fierce* in the dictionary, you'll see adjectives such as "strong," "powerful," "aggressive," and even "savage." That definition makes me think of the wild cats of Africa and India—untamed, dangerous, beautiful, and so powerful. When we hear this description of *fierce*, it may not fit our image of what a beautiful woman of God should be. It may sound too intense or even masculine. But under God's control, a fierce woman of God is a beautiful warrior—not savage or violent but powerful and dangerous in the best sense of the word.

During this six-week study, we are going to dig into fierce women of God in the Bible who lived courageously, obediently, and faithfully in order to fulfill God's plan. Their stories show us the power that comes from resting in God's love and forgiveness—and how this power can lead to amazing things as we lean into His plans for each of us. When we think of fierce women in the Bible, we tend to think of well-known women such as Sarah, Rachel, Ruth, Esther, and Mary, the mother of Jesus. But in these lessons we will be looking at some lesser-known female characters of the Bible, such as the midwives of Egypt, Shiphrah and Puah, and Lois and Eunice. Why? Because these women were heroines too. They show us that the faithfulness of ordinary women can change the world. In fact, fierce women such as these have been changing the world for thousands of years. Many have received little recognition, but they lived fiercely anyway. And we can too!

This workbook contains six weeks' worth of devotional Bible lessons, with five lessons for each week. I call them devotional lessons because they include both Scripture study as well as reflection and prayer. I hope you'll give yourself the gift of time alone with God to savor His Word and allow Him to speak to you. You may want to find a quiet place—maybe your favorite chair or a spot on the porch, weather permitting—where you can spend your devotional study time.

Each day the lesson follows the same format:

Settle: As you begin each lesson, I encourage you to just be still for a few moments and allow your heart and mind to settle. In Psalm 46:10 we are told to "be still, and know that I am God!" In the fast-paced world in which most of us operate, being still, breathing deeply, and resting in God's presence can be challenging. So, I encourage you as you begin each day's lesson to give yourself the sweet treasure of settling your heart, mind, and soul into your heavenly Father's presence. This alone can be a life changer as you go through the study!

Focus: Next, focus your mind on God's Word, reading a thematic verse and a Scripture from the main story for the day. Isaiah 55:10-11 (TLB) has a promise for those who dwell on God's Word:

*As the rain and snow come down from heaven and stay upon the ground
to water the earth, and cause the grain to grow and to produce seed for the
farmer and bread for the hungry, so also is my word. I send it out, and
it always produces fruit. It shall accomplish all I want it to and prosper
everywhere I send it.*

Reflect: Now it's time to get to the story and think about how it speaks into your life. God's Word is so rich, and the stories of biblical heroines have so much to teach us. The lessons, triumphs, and tragedies of their lives are relevant to us today. As you consider their stories, some may be familiar to you. Try to look at them with new eyes. Invite God to give you fresh insights to enrich your life. Space is provided for recording your responses and completing exercises.

Pray: Finally, be still once again and enter into a time of prayer, asking the Holy Spirit to speak new truths of peace and wisdom into your life. I will offer a few prayer suggestions each day—and occasionally a written prayer that you may pray word for word or adapt as your own—to help your time with God be fresh and interesting.

As you begin and end each day's lesson, I encourage you to be creative in your approach to connecting with God. He is a creative genius; just look at the giraffe, butterfly, and anteater! Obviously, God likes variety and creativity. At times I will encourage you to try some new things in the "Settle" and "Pray" segments of the lessons. For instance, if you're musical, you may want to begin by singing or playing an instrument. If you're artistic, you may want to end each day by sketching or painting. Perhaps your gift is the written word; then journal what God is speaking to you. You also may want to incorporate praise and worship music (I have included a few song suggestions, but feel free to choose your own) as well as dance or stretching and other physical activity into your devotional study time. Be creative! Think outside your usual practices and try something new.

Before you get started, gather all the supplies you'll need: your Bible, this workbook, a pen or pencil, and any items you need for creative expression—such as a journal, a sketch pad, an instrument, or a device and playlist. Have your tools easily accessible so that nothing deters your time. Another trick I've found helpful is to have a notepad handy so that if your thoughts begin to drift to things you need to do later, you can just jot them down so they do not steal your time with God.

Now, let me tell you in advance, I want to be a fierce woman of God. And I want you to be one also! When we live with this strong sense of knowing who we are in Christ, we have the courage to live obediently and faithfully into His great, big plans! And women like that change the world.

Let's be fierce!

Jen

Week 1

Shiphrah and Puah

Exodus 1

DAY 1

Settle

Find your favorite spot. As you settle in, take a deep breath and lift your hands over your head, holding the breath a few seconds. Then slowly exhale, lowering your hands. Do this a few times, allowing your heart and mind to calm as you focus your thoughts on God.

Focus

[1]*These are the names of the sons of Israel (that is, Jacob) who moved to Egypt with their father, each with his family:* [2]*Reuben, Simeon, Levi, Judah,* [3]*Issachar, Zebulun, Benjamin,* [4]*Dan, Naphtali, Gad, and Asher.* [5]*In all, Jacob had seventy descendants in Egypt, including Joseph, who was already there.*

[6]*In time, Joseph and all of his brothers died, ending that entire generation.* [7]*But their descendants, the Israelites, had many children and grandchildren. In fact, they multiplied so greatly that they became extremely powerful and filled the land.*

[8]*Eventually, a new king came to power in Egypt who knew nothing about Joseph or what he had done.* [9]*He said to his people, "Look, the people of Israel now outnumber us and are stronger than we are.* [10]*We must make a plan to keep them from growing even more. If we don't, and if war breaks out, they will join our enemies and fight against us. Then they will escape from the country."*

[11]*So the Egyptians made the Israelites their slaves. They appointed brutal slave drivers over them, hoping to wear them down with crushing labor. They forced them to build the cities of Pithom and Rameses as supply centers for the king.* [12]*But the more the Egyptians oppressed them, the more the Israelites multiplied and spread, and the more alarmed the Egyptians became.* [13]*So the Egyptians worked the people of Israel without mercy.* [14]*They made their lives bitter, forcing them to mix mortar and make bricks and do all the work in the fields. They were ruthless in all their demands.*

[15]*Then Pharaoh, the king of Egypt, gave this order to the Hebrew midwives, Shiphrah and Puah:* [16]*"When you help the Hebrew women as they give birth, watch as they deliver. If the baby is a boy, kill him; if it is a girl,*

let her live." [17]*But because the midwives feared God, they refused to obey the king's orders. They allowed the boys to live, too.*

(Exodus 1:1-17)

Reflect

Sarah, Mary, Anna, and Rachel are familiar biblical names. In fact, you probably know someone with each of these names. But what about Shiphrah and Puah? These are not well-known women of the Bible. We don't name our babies after these heroines. Perhaps that's because theirs is a tough story. Or maybe it is because they have only a brief mention in the beginning of Exodus. But their story is one worth knowing. It is powerful. It is fierce.

During the time of the famine in Israel, Joseph, who had risen to become a prince of Egypt, invited the Hebrews to come and settle in the area of Egypt known as Goshen. During their time in Egypt, the Israelites multiplied and flourished. In fact, they flourished so much that the new pharaoh was threatened by their numbers and ordered the women who assisted with the birthing process, the midwives, to kill all the male infants immediately at birth.

Do you know anyone who works as a midwife—or perhaps as an OB/GYN or labor and delivery nurse? I do, and these women love people—children in particular. It's part of why they chose the profession. They know that to be part of the birthing process is to see God's work at its finest. It's the opportunity to see miracles on a daily basis. Their jobs are to bring health and healing to those they serve.

Now imagine these women you know being ordered to kill the very miracles they have just witnessed being born. It's a disgusting image. Truly evil! Surely, any good midwife, nurse, or doctor would cringe at this type of command. Shiphrah and Puah did!

Reread Exodus 1:15-17 (pages 13–14). What did Shiphrah and Puah do in response to the king's command?

They allowed the boys to live! What an act of courage; what fierce faithfulness to the God they served. Their fear of the Lord and His laws took precedence over what an earthly ruler commanded them to do. Surely, they must have imagined what a king who ordered genocide could have done to them if he came to know his orders had been defied. Surely, they were afraid. But even in their fear, they were faithful.

Let's talk about our fears. They are real, and we all have them. In fact, psychologists have discovered hundreds of known fears that plague us. Some fears even grow to the point of becoming phobias, such as:

Ablutophobia	the fear of bathing (My son had that one for a while as a little kid!)
Ergophobia	the fear of work (Have you ever had a coworker with this? I have!)
Nomophobia	the fear of being without a mobile phone (Can you relate?)
Ophidiophobia	the fear of snakes (That's just good sense in my opinion!)
Omphalophobia	the fear of belly buttons (One-piece bathing suits only for these folks.)
Phobophobia	the fear of fear (Check it out; it's a real thing.)

Now, here's the thing about fear: it may seem silly to you, unless it's your particular issue. Because when it's your deal, it's real. No matter whether the fear is substantiated or not, there is good news: you don't have to be afraid; God is on your side!

What fears do you face on a recurring basis? *Fear of criticism or criticism of my beliefs — fear of emotional attack.*

How do these fears affect your daily life? *I "brace" myself too much*

How have these fears affected your relationship with God?

What shall we say about such wonderful things as these? If God is for us, who can ever be against us?

  (Romans 8:31)

Read Romans 8:31 in the margin. What does this verse teach us about facing our fears?

Fear is not of God but of the enemy of our souls, whose game plan is to steal, kill, and destroy (John 10:10)—to rob us of joy and keep us from being faithful to God. Giving in to our fears keeps us from living our best lives and becoming the beautiful warriors of God that we are designed to be.

In my life, the fear of failure and criticism has, at times, paralyzed me. It's like a snake (which I hate) slithering in front of me, keeping me from taking the next step. These fears of human rejection have, occasionally, kept me from following Jesus closely, stealing the joy and peace that come from doing life in God's will.

What fear has paralyzed you in the past? *Fear of failure or rejection, fear of gaining weight*

What fear has been most destructive in your life?

Fear of not being pure and perfect, "Scrupulosity" is phobic fear of God.

Shiphrah and Puah were human, which means that they too had fears; but they chose to honor God even when they were afraid. Their fear of God was greater than their fear of an earthly ruler. And as we will see throughout this week, God rewarded their faithfulness.

It's important to note that a healthy fear of God is different from phobic fear. Theologian Robert B. Strimple says that as we fear God, "There is the convergence of awe, reverence, adoration, honor, worship, confidence, thankfulness, love, and, yes, fear."[1] When we read about the fear of God in the Bible, it is appropriate in most cases to replace *fear* with *honor* or *reverence*. Consider Psalm 145:19, for example:

He grants the desires of those who fear him;
>   he hears their cries for help and rescues them.
He grants the desires of those who **honor/reverence** him;
>   he hears their cries for help and rescues them.

A healthy fear of God helps to direct our paths.

However, there also is fear of the judgment of God. The midwives most likely feared God in both of these aspects.

have love and reverence for

Look up these verses on the fear of God, and write your thoughts about each in the space provided:

Psalm 33:18 *In times of crisis we can place our hope in God*

Psalm 34:7 *"The angel of the Lord encamps around those who fear him and delivers them"*

Proverbs 15:16

Luke 1:50

A healthy fear of God helps to direct our paths, and when we are faced with difficult choices, it can help to guide us. Every day we are faced with challenges. Every day is an opportunity to live for Christ. But in order to do that, we must settle in advance who will be in control of our lives—even when that means making a difficult choice. Romans 6:12-13 reminds us, "Do not let sin control the way you live; do not give in to sinful desires. . . . Instead, give yourselves completely to God, for you were dead, but now you have new life. So use your whole body as an instrument to do what is right for the glory of God."

Through the rest of the week we will dig into the story of Shiprah and Puah and the fierce way they lived out their faith during national genocide. We will see that they were women of quiet strength, fearless determination, and faithful resolve who received great blessings from God for their obedience. May we seek to be women who live in this fierce manner!

Pray

- Spend a few minutes in worship, thanking God for who He is.
- Ask God to reveal to you the earthly fears that keep you from living into His will for your life.
- Surrender your agenda to His today.

DAY 2

Settle

Take time to count your blessings as you begin your intentional time with God today. Think back to when you were a little girl, and write a list of ten to twenty ways that God has showered His goodness upon you throughout your lifetime. As you write these, make them a prayer of thanksgiving.

Focus

But because the midwives feared God, they refused to obey the king's orders.
They allowed the boys to live, too.

(*Exodus* 1:17)

Who are those who fear the LORD?
    He will show them the path they should choose.

(*Psalm* 25:12)

The fear of human opinion disables;
    trusting in God protects you from that.

(*Proverbs* 29:25 MSG)

Reflect

When I was seventeen years old, I went on a mission trip and heard God call me into ministry. I didn't hear an audible voice, but it was very clear to me that God was calling me to be in ministry. It was a sweet and precious moment. God's favor and love were present in a powerful way, though I had no idea at the time what that meant. Having grown up in church, I observed that most of the women I had seen in ministry were children's leaders or women who had remained single and dedicated their whole lives to serving the church. They were wonderful people with wonderful ministries, but their particular roles didn't seem to be what God was calling me to. I felt a calling to teach adults by sharing God's truths through speaking and writing. Yet I thought that wouldn't work because, if I'm honest, I had heard a good bit of criticism about women

Fierce women have a strength that comes from beyond themselves.

in ministry; and frankly, I didn't want that coming at me. So, I did nothing.

Fast-forward two years. I was sitting in a business law class when God spoke to me again. But this time it wasn't as sweet and precious. It was more of a spanking. I'm speaking figuratively here to make a point. It was a spanking in the sense of conviction. This time God said, "Jen, what are you doing? Why aren't you leaning into my will?" Have you ever had a loving God-whipping like that? They sting a little!

I needed God to understand—I had my reasons. You see, Jim and I were dating seriously, and he was going into the ministry. *Both people in a marriage can't be ministry leaders*, I thought. Now, from time to time I would mention the ministry idea to others, but most people told me that it just wouldn't work. "Let him do the ministry," they would say. They told me I should pursue teaching or business or really anything else. After all, I was a woman.

I continued to hear God speak to my heart, and I found ways to serve behind the scenes. Children's and youth ministries, missions, and administration all seemed acceptable. My fears of what others would think or say about me if I stepped into the role of teacher or speaker paralyzed me. So again, I did nothing.

Then God took me to the woodshed again, asking again why I hadn't pursued the calling He had given me. After that a new thought occurred to me—*What if I miss out on what God has planned for me*? And this thought far outweighed whatever gossip or criticism could come my way.

Now, I should tell you that I'm not a feminist in the sense that some interpret the word. I have no ax to grind. Some of my favorite people are men—just ask my husband, dad, and son! Men play a powerful and extraordinary role in God's grand scheme. So do women. I'm also not a doormat. Women with strong personalities and leadership roles are changing the world. So, what am I? Just a woman wanting to be obedient to God and fulfill His plans for me.

That's when I began to lean in—lean in to how God created me, lean in to my gifts and strengths. And there I found new joy and purpose. I've also faced criticism, and in those moments I've experienced hurt and discouragement; but there have been no more trips to the woodshed related to this issue, and for that I am thankful.

At some point, my fear of missing out on all that God has for me became greater than the earthly consequences I would face if I was obedient to God. This released a powerful freedom in my life. A fierceness to live into God's plan developed within me.

There is something ironically beautiful about a feminine warrior—someone who can be soft and strong, gentle and ferocious.

Reread Proverbs 29:25 (page 19). How has human opinion influenced you recently?

Whose opinions of you do you fear? *My church friends*

How does this fear impact your life? *It inhibits me*

How does trusting in God protect you from the impact of other people's opinions? *If God loves me I know that is the most important thing*

Fierce women have a strength that comes from beyond themselves. They are bathed in the forgiveness and love of Jesus. He holds their hearts so firmly that they are able to find joy and peace in the midst of their battles. These women find their identity in Christ, which provides them with a courage and fortitude that outweighs the fears they face. Fierce women of God are warriors at heart—not savage or violent but tempered with loving-kindness. They are beautiful servants with backbones made of steel. They are wise, gentle, and dangerous—in the best sense of those words.

I love to see God's fierce women in action. God wants all of His girls to live with a fierce faithfulness, as we see in Scripture. Deborah led the army of God (Judges 4–5). Esther stood up to a potential annihilation of her people (Esther 4–7). Priscilla and Lydia led and served in a time when women held little value (1 Corinthians 16:19 and Acts 16:12-15). All are fierce examples of how God uses those who are available to Him.

Our heroines this week are just as noble. Shiphrah and Puah, the two midwives mentioned by name in Exodus 1, had a choice to make. Would they live out Pharaoh's evil command to kill all the male children, or would they disobey, risking their lives?

Reread Exodus 1:17, which we also read yesterday (page 19). According to this verse, why did Shiphrah and Puah refuse to obey the king?

Though this Egyptian king was willing to commit genocide to secure his power, the women were willing to risk their lives in order to honor God by valuing human life. What would he have done to the midwives had their plot been uncovered? They chose well in spite of the danger.

You too will face difficult decisions—though I hope not as evil as those the midwives faced. May these six steps from Proverbs help you face them with courage and fierce faithfulness:

1. **Pray.** First, and above all else, seek God's will.

   Whoever trusts in his own mind is a fool,
   but he who walks in wisdom will be delivered.
   (*Proverbs* 28:26 ESV)

2. **Gather the facts.** Be sure you have accurate information before making a decision.

   Get the facts at any price, and hold on tightly to all the good sense you can get.

   (*Proverbs* 23:23 TLB)

3. **Seek godly advice.** There is great wisdom in consulting with mature believers.

> *Don't go to war without wise guidance;*
> > *victory depends on having many advisers.*
> > > (Proverbs 24:6)

4. **Consider the consequences.** Every decision has repercussions. What will it gain and cost?

> *It is foolish and rash to make a promise to the Lord before counting the cost.*
> > (Proverbs 20:25 TLB)

5. **Prepare for difficulties.** Anticipate problems that may arise.

> *A prudent person foresees dangers and takes precautions.*
> > *The simpleton goes blindly on and suffers the consequences.*
> > > (Proverbs 22:3)

6. **Face your fears.** Fierce warriors aren't unafraid; they are just willing to face their fears and move anyway.

> *Fearing people is a dangerous trap,*
> > *but trusting the LORD means safety.*
> > > (Proverbs 29:25)

Which of these six steps do you do well?

Where do you stumble?

How can you prepare so that you won't stumble there in the future?

> God calls on you to be fierce and faithful in standing up for His Word and His values.

God wants to use you just as He used Shiphrah, Puah, Deborah, Lydia, and so many others throughout history. God calls on you to be fierce and faithful in standing up for His Word and His values. Jesus invites you to rest in His love as a gentle warrior. Face whatever has held you back in the past in order to be fully usable for His purposes today.

Pray

- Pray the following prayer, or craft your own prayer thanking God for His patience and tenacity in using people like us for His purposes:

Heavenly Father, thank You for loving me so passionately. Help me to understand that depth of love and to be filled with it so that I can extend it back to You and splash it onto those around me. As I face difficult decisions, give me wisdom and courage to live in a way that pleases You. May I be used for Your purposes today. In the name and power of Jesus. Amen.

DAY 3

Settle

Psalm 46:10 reads, "Be still, and know that I am God!" Allow this verse to guide you as you calm your thoughts and focus on God. If there are things troubling you, write them down and put them aside for the next few minutes in order to give God your full attention.

Focus

¹⁵*Then Pharaoh, the king of Egypt, gave this order to the Hebrew midwives, Shiphrah and Puah:* ¹⁶*"When you help the Hebrew women as they give birth, watch as they deliver. If the baby is a boy, kill him; if it is a girl, let her live."* ¹⁷*But because the midwives feared God, they refused to obey the king's orders. They allowed the boys to live, too.*

(Exodus 1:15-17)

⁶*In time, Joseph and all of his brothers died, ending that entire generation.* ⁷*But their descendants, the Israelites, had many children and grandchildren. In fact, they multiplied so greatly that they became extremely powerful and filled the land.*

⁸*Eventually, a new king came to power in Egypt who knew nothing about Joseph or what he had done.* ⁹*He said to his people, "Look, the people of Israel now outnumber us and are stronger than we are.* ¹⁰*We must make a plan to keep them from growing even more. If we don't, and if war breaks out, they will join our enemies and fight against us. Then they will escape from the country."*

¹¹*So the Egyptians made the Israelites their slaves. They appointed brutal slave drivers over them, hoping to wear them down with crushing labor. They forced them to build the cities of Pithom and Rameses as supply centers for the king.* ¹²*But the more the Egyptians oppressed them, the more the Israelites multiplied and spread, and the more alarmed the Egyptians became.* ¹³*So the Egyptians worked the people of Israel without mercy.* ¹⁴*They made their lives bitter, forcing them to mix mortar and make bricks and do all the work in the fields. They were ruthless in all their demands.*

(Exodus 1:6-14)

Don't let evil conquer you, but conquer evil by doing good.

(Romans 12:21)

Dear children, let's not merely say that we love each other; let us show the truth by our actions.

(1 John 3:18)

Reflect

Do you know the name Irena Sendlerowa (also known as Irena Sendler)? During World War II this young woman found herself in a unique position. She was a social worker in Poland when almost four hundred thousand Jews were herded into a small ghetto camp and forced to live in cramped, unhygienic conditions. It was reported that as many as four thousand people a month perished from starvation and disease there. Irena, along with other Polish caregivers, brought aid to those suffering in the ghetto through food and medical care. But as the conditions deteriorated and the Nazis began to deport Jews to concentration camps, Irena and about two dozen colleagues knew they must do more. So they took action. At great personal risk, they began to find ways to smuggle infants and children out of the ghetto and place them in non-Jewish families to give them a chance at life.

Through means such as ambulances, sewer systems, coffins, and even toolboxes, over twenty-five hundred children were brought to freedom. Her love for God moved her to become involved—to courageously and faithfully do what she could to protect those who could not protect themselves. She shared about what led her to action:

> When the war started, all of Poland was drowning in a sea of blood. But most of all, it affected the Jewish nation. And within that nation, it was the children who suffered most. That's why we needed to give our hearts to them. . . .
> We did these things as completely normal things, on the principle that when a person is drowning, we should reach out a hand to them, or at least a pinky finger.[2]

Just like Puah and Shiphrah, Irena could not sit idly by and comply with evil. From the time that Joseph first made a home for the Israelites in Egypt, God had blessed them; and their numbers had grown into the millions. The strength of the Hebrew nation threatened the Egyptian pharaoh, so he set out to commit genocide against them.

Reread Exodus 1:10 (page 25). What were Pharaoh's specific fears?

History is littered with evil leaders who sought to annihilate those who might oppose their power. What examples come to your mind? Mao   Hitler

Hutus   Stalin

Irena Sendlerowa and the Egyptian midwives were uniquely placed in history to courageously take action in desperate times. Now, we know the story of Moses, and we've have heard of Oskar Schindler, made famous by Steven Spielberg's award-winning film *Schindler's List*. But these three women—Irena, Shiphrah, and Puah—received little fanfare in their time. Even so, their stories are fierce. Their bravery in the face of great evil saved the lives of many—and they did this knowing that their very lives were at risk.

In fact, in 1943 Irena was arrested and tortured at Gestapo headquarters in Warsaw. She never revealed any information, though her legs and feet were broken during interrogation. She was sentenced to death, but on the way to her execution the driver, who had been bribed by Jewish underground aid workers, beat her and left her on the side of the road. After recovering from her injuries, Irena returned to her efforts to help as many children as possible. She never considered herself a hero—just a follower of God doing what she could to help all she could.[3]

Irena Sendlerowa died in Poland in 2008 at the age of ninety-eight.[4] Though she may not have considered herself a hero, the twenty-five hundred children she saved surely must believe otherwise.

We truly love others when we put aside our own needs and fears and stand for those who cannot stand for themselves.

As God's girls we have the opportunity to bring light into the darkness.

What situations in our world seem unjust to you?

How can you speak up for and protect those who can't speak for themselves?

Edmund Burke is famously quoted as saying, "The only thing necessary for the triumph of evil is for good men to do nothing."[5] Of course, this goes for women too. Our heroines this week, Shiphrah and Puah, took a stand. Like Irena Sendlerowa, they had to work carefully and with God's guidance in order to make a difference in a time of crisis. Our planet faces crises of similar proportions today as well.

What is our responsibility as Christ followers to respond to the injustices in our world?

Dear children, let's not merely say that we love each other; let us show the truth by our actions.
(1 John 3:18)

Read 1 John 3:18 and Romans 13:1 in the margin. How do we reconcile these two verses?

Everyone must submit to governing authorities. For all authority comes from God, and those in positions of authority have been placed there by God.
(Romans 13:1)

How has God prompted you to take action in the past? What did you do?

To help with Family Promise, Bashor Children's Home

As Christ followers, we know that the greatest commands of Jesus are to love God and to love one another (Matthew 22:37-39). This kind of love is more than a feeling. It is not just hoping and praying for the best. We don't practice love only when we feel goosebumps. Love is a decision and action, as we read in 1 John 3:18. And this love is commanded of us, as we read in the Gospels: "So now I am giving you a new commandment:

Love each other. Just as I have loved you, you should love each other" (John 13:34).

We truly love others when, with courage, we put aside our own needs and fears and stand for those who cannot stand for themselves. As I think of modern-day women who are doing this, I think of those who work in missions, those who are foster parents, and those who deliver Bibles in places where Christianity is not welcome.

As we read Exodus 1, Pharaoh's edict seems barbaric, but similar laws have existed in our time. In China, where there was a one-child-per-family law for many years (outlawed in 2016), it was the baby girls who often were victims of infanticide or abandonment. And in many countries there are still barbaric practices related to women and children. Such realities are abhorrent to those of us who value God's law and the preciousness of human life. What will we do? How can we respond? Can we make a difference? These are the same questions that Shiphrah and Puah surely must have asked themselves. The consequences of disobedience were death, but they chose to love God and love others faithfully, and to put that faith into action.

Like the midwives of Egypt, modern-day heroines continue to serve God. Often their work goes on quietly, and they may receive little recognition on this side of heaven. But, oh, what mansions there must be awaiting them in heaven!

Friends, it's difficult to write this devotional lesson because it touches on unlovely things—concentration camps, families ripped apart, and genocide. There is evil in our world. But as God's girls we have the opportunity to bring light into the darkness. May we live fiercely determined to shine love where there is hate and bring hope where there is injustice, just as the midwives of Egypt did.

Pray

- As you come into God's presence through prayer, take a few moments just to worship. Thank Him for His majesty and righteousness.
- Ask God to give you a heart that breaks for what breaks His.
- Ask God for wisdom and practical steps in how He would have you respond to the injustices in our world.

DAY 4

Settle

Begin your time with God in a creative way today. Draw, sing, write, take a short walk—whatever you choose, do it with God. Spend this creative energy focused on God's goodness, and let your activity be a form of worshiping Him.

Focus

But the midwives had far too much respect for God and didn't do what the king of Egypt ordered; they let the boy babies live.

(Exodus 1:17 MSG)

Peter and the apostles replied, "We must obey God rather than any human authority. The God of our ancestors raised Jesus from the dead after you killed him by hanging him on a cross. Then God put Him in the place of honor at His right hand. . . ." The apostles left the high council rejoicing that God had counted them worthy to suffer disgrace for the name of Jesus.

(Acts 5:29-31, 41)

(Read the full account of Peter before the Sanhedrin in Acts 5:12-41.)

For we are not fighting against flesh-and-blood enemies, but against evil rulers and authorities of the unseen world, against mighty powers in this dark world, and against evil spirits in the heavenly places.

Therefore, put on every piece of God's armor so you will be able to resist the enemy in the time of evil. Then after the battle you will still be standing firm. Stand your ground.

(Ephesians 6:12-14a)

Reflect

In general, I'm a rule follower. Detention after school, writing sentences, and being grounded were not part of my story when I was growing up. So when I was called to the principal's office my freshman year of high school, it was newsworthy among my friends. They were shocked. But it was not a surprise to me—I knew what I had done.

Here's what happened. I had a government class first thing every day. For some odd reason, in this class I ended up being the only girl in a group of about twenty-five. It was a crass group of guys, and the teacher (a male coach) thought their teasing and coarse humor was funny. Today we would call it harassment; back then it was just thought of as "guys being guys." But without sharing too many details, it was wrong. For months I endured a really inappropriate situation. On the day of our final, I—with the help of my mother, I might add—brought the guys a treat: chocolate chip cookies made with chocolate Ex-Lax. It brought me great joy to watch them, coach included, gobble those tasty treats down.

At the end of the test I got up, stood in the front of the room, and said, "Guys, those treats are exactly what you deserve. You have been horrible to me. I'm pleased to let you know there is no real chocolate in those cookies; it's Ex-Lax. Enjoy your day." And then it got awesome, friends!

One by one they began to check out of school, and by lunch time I found myself in the vice principal's office. He was a really wise man; his wife was actually my Sunday school teacher, which helped me that day for sure. He talked sternly to me in the hallway and then had me come into his office where he burst out laughing and gave me a high five.

I should probably regret serving those cookies, but I don't.

Rules are meant to be followed. In fact, there are Scriptures to guide us in this regard:

> *Obey your leaders and submit to them, for they are keeping watch over your souls, as those who will have to give an account. Let them do this with joy and not with groaning, for that would be of no advantage to you.*
>
> (Hebrews 13:17 ESV)

> *Everyone must submit to governing authorities.*
>
> (Romans 13:1)

However, when we read accounts such as that of the midwives Puah and Shiphrah, we are met with a conundrum. How do we make sense of this? Is there a contradiction here? This is where wisdom must prevail. In the first chapter of Exodus we are reminded that God's law always comes before human law. We are not taught to be blindly submissive.

There is a time to submit, and there is a time to stand.

There is a time to submit, and there is a time to stand. When God's law is clearly violated, as is the case here with a command to murder infants, we cannot pretend we have no responsibility.

Reread Exodus 1:17 in *The Message* (page 30). How does this verse illustrate Puah's and Shiphrah's respect for God's law?

How does our respect or disrespect for God influence our daily decisions?

The midwives valued God's favor more than they did Pharaoh's. They feared God's wrath more than they did the wrath of Egyptian rule. Their motivation came from a deep and abiding love for God's standards and for the value of God's created life. They refused to obey evil. And as we will see tomorrow, they were rewarded for their courageous obedience.

This passage from Exodus does not teach us to reject ethical authority. It is not an excuse for children to rebel against their parents or for us to overturn governments. But it does make one point clear: submission to civil authorities has limits. Centuries later when Peter is arrested and stands before the Jewish authorities, they order him to no longer preach the good news of Christ. Upon hearing these orders he boldly proclaims, "We must obey God rather than human authority" (Acts 5:29).

Turn again to Acts 5:12-42. What lessons do you extract from this confrontation between the apostles and the Jewish leaders?

How might history be different if Peter and the other apostles had complied with the Sanhedrin's order to never again teach in Jesus' name?

How might history be different if Shiphrah and Puah had complied with Pharaoh's edict?

As we learn to walk in God's strength we will be empowered to do great things.

It would be naive to think that there may not be consequences when we take a stand. Peter faced hardships, just as Paul, James, and even Jesus did. But they chose to stand anyway. When faced with difficulties, it is good to remember who is our true enemy.

Read Ephesians 6:11 in the margin. Who is our true enemy?

Put on all of God's armor so that you will be able to stand firm against all strategies of the devil. (Ephesians 6:11)

To me, Ephesians 6 is one of the most powerful passages in the Bible. This chapter outlines beautifully what we are up against and how we are to defend ourselves and our faith. It instructs us to put on the whole armor of God and promises that then we will be able to stand in our struggles.

Read Ephesians 6:10-18 and describe in your own words how we are fitted for battle:

Belt =

Breastplate =

Shoes =

Shield =

Helmet =

Sword =

With which of these do you need to dress yourself more carefully? How can you accomplish that?

It has been thousands of years since Shiphrah and Puah walked the earth and made the decision to quietly stand against evil. A lot has changed in these years, but a lot is very much the same. Evil is alive and well, and that is cause for us to rise daily and dress ourselves in God's armor so that we may stand—fierce, strong, and effective as God's daughters. Friends, as we learn to walk in God's strength—not ahead of His will and not lagging behind it—we will be empowered to do great things in our lifetime. May we unleash the influence and power of the Holy Spirit as we follow Him fiercely!

Pray

- Listen to Jasmine Murray's recording of the song "Fearless" (or another relevant song of your choice).
- Ask God to give you courage to stand for His laws with strength and gentleness.
- Lift up the concerns of your heart to God and trust Him to care for you.

DAY 5

Settle

Take a deep breath or two and allow your mind to slow and your thoughts to center on Christ. Repeat the name of Jesus several times, and allow His presence to invade your space as you begin your time with Him today.

Focus

[15]Then Pharaoh, the king of Egypt, gave this order to the Hebrew midwives, Shiphrah and Puah: [16]"When you help the Hebrew women as they give birth, watch as they deliver. If the baby is a boy, kill him; if it is a girl, let her live." [17]But because the midwives feared God, they refused to obey the king's orders. They allowed the boys to live, too.

[18]So the king of Egypt called for the midwives. "Why have you done this?" he demanded. "Why have you allowed the boys to live?"

[19]"The Hebrew women are not like the Egyptian women," the midwives replied. "They are more vigorous and have their babies so quickly that we cannot get there in time."

[20]So God was good to the midwives, and the Israelites continued to multiply, growing more and more powerful. [21]And because the midwives feared God, he gave them families of their own.

(Exodus 1:15-21)

[1]Blessed is the one
    who does not walk in step with the wicked
or stand in the way that sinners take
    or sit in the company of mockers,
[2]but whose delight is in the law of the Lord,
    and who meditates on his law day and night.
[3]That person is like a tree planted by streams of water,
    which yields its fruit in season
and whose leaf does not wither—
    whatever they do prospers.

(Psalm 1:1-3 NIV)

God masters in turning what may seem ordinary to us into the extraordinary when under His control.

Reflect

As we look back on history, those who jump out at us are often inventors, rulers, explorers, and military leaders. These are the people most often credited with changing the course of history. Their contributions are often heroic for they discovered unknown worlds, created new technologies, and paved the way for peace in times of war. Heroes in the form of midwives, on the other hand, are unexpected. But isn't that just like God? He masters in turning what may seem ordinary to us into the extraordinary when under His control. The Bible is filled with unexpected heroes: a shepherd boy turned king, David; a young minority girl turned queen, Esther; a fisherman turned evangelical preacher, Peter. These are ordinary lives that changed the world through the power of God at work in them.

This week our study has been on two unlikely heroes, Shiphrah and Puah. As we've seen, they are the midwives mentioned by name at the beginning of Exodus who would not obey Pharaoh's wicked order to kill all of the newborn boys. Their courage to obey God's law above human law honored God and, as we read in today's passage, they were rewarded for that faithfulness:

> [20]*So God was good to the midwives, and the Israelites continued to multiply, growing more and more powerful.* [21]*And because the midwives feared God, he gave them families of their own.*
>
> (*Exodus* 1:20-21)

Reread the verses above and consider the spiritual and emotional rewards you have received from walking in God's favor.

In the King James Version of the Bible we read verse 21 slightly differently: "And it came to pass, because the midwives feared God, that he made them houses." Although there is some disagreement as to whether the blessing of family means that they personally had many children or whether they established a long and rich legacy in their family trees through their influence, the implication is the same. They were rewarded for their fierce faithfulness. God honored these two women and blessed them for their faithful actions during a time of crisis for His people.

We, too, are faced with opportunities to compromise our values. In business, ethical standards are often disregarded to pad the bottom line. Sex outside of the marriage relationship is common. And the love of success in the world's eyes often outweighs the love of success in God's eyes. How will we respond when these issues present themselves in our lives?

What temptations to compromise do we face as Christians today?

When have you experienced a conflict of your values? How did you respond?

Toward the end of the apostle Peter's life, he wrote a beautiful letter of encouragement to the followers of Christ. At this time many of them were suffering for their faith. In order to live out their faith they had to make difficult choices.

Read 1 Peter 3:13-17. How have you personally suffered from doing good?

Verse 16 instructs us to keep our conscience clear so that others will be ashamed when they speak against us. What practical steps can you to take to live above reproach in order to keep your conscience clear?

The blessings we receive from following God do not always come in the forms we may expect.

What sets Puah and Shiphrah apart is that in a dangerous and difficult situation they were courageously faithful. They quietly chose to honor God first in their lives, and in return God blessed them. Galatians 6:9 reads, "And let us not grow weary of doing good, for in due season we will reap, if we do not give up" (ESV). This is a promise from God that as we continue to serve Him we will reap a blessing. Similarly, Proverbs 28:20 tells us that "the trustworthy person will get a rich reward." The blessings we receive from following God do not always come in the forms we may expect. Sometimes they are tangible; at other times they come in the form of spiritual or emotional maturity. God's blessings sometimes come in exactly the way we had hoped, but often we have to trust that God is at work even when we don't see it—even when we do not immediately recognize how He may choose to reward us when we are faithful.

Scripture tells us that Shiphrah and Puah were rewarded richly for honoring Him. God saw their faithfulness, and He blessed them with many children and a rich legacy—a legacy so rich, in fact, that here we are spending a week of devotionals studying about them thousands of years later.

When have you obeyed God's law in a difficult situation and later experienced His blessings in your life—spiritual/emotional or tangible?

Isn't it awesome that God would take two simple midwives and use them in such an incredible way? This is God's specialty—taking ordinary people and using them in extraordinary ways. I don't know about you, but I consider myself a pretty ordinary person, and it's exciting to think that God could use me, too, in extraordinary ways. How does that happen? It's through fierce obedience and faithfulness. May we, like Puah and Shiphrah, be fiercely courageous and live into the extraordinary callings that God has for us; and then may we enjoy the blessings that He will shower upon us!

Pray

- Thank God for the blessings in your life. Name them and praise Him for His goodness.
- Lift up to God issues of injustice in our world.
- Ask God to give you courage to stand for His principles even in challenging circumstances.

Then Pharoah, the king of Egypt, gave this order to the Hebrew midwives, Shiphrah and Puah: "When you help the Hebrew women as they give birth, watch as they deliver. If the baby is a boy, kill him; it if is a girl, let her live.' But because the midwives feared God, they refused to obey the king's orders. They allowed the boys to live, too." (Exodus 1:15-17)

When I am afraid,
I will put my trust in You.
In God, whose word I praise.
        (Psalm 56:3-4a NASB)

There is neither Jew nor Greek, there is neither slave nor free, there is no male and female, for you are all one in Christ Jesus. (Galatians 3:28 ESV)

We have to be sure that our leadership is under God's _____.

The *fear of human opinion disables;*
    trusting in GOD *protects you from that.*
        (Proverbs 29:25 MSG)

It's important that we become _____ of our fears so that we can _____ them through prayer and practical steps as the Lord directs.

Fierce women of God will face _____.

God was kind to the midwives and the people increased and became even more numerous. And because the midwives feared God, he gave them families of their own. (Exodus 1:20-21 NIV)

God dealt well with the midwives . . . And it came to pass, because the midwives feared God, that he made them houses. (Exodus 1:20-21 KJV)

God rewards _____—sometimes tangibly but always spiritually.

"Well done, good and faithful servant. You have been faithful over a little; I will set you over much. Enter into the joy of your master." (Matthew 25:21 ESV)

Week 2

Deborah

Judges 4–5

DAY 1

Settle

If possible, find a new spot today for your time with God. Mix it up a little so that you stay alert and fresh as you enter into God's presence. Come before God with an expectation that He is going to move in your life during this time.

Focus

¹After Ehud's death, the Israelites again did evil in the LORD's sight. ²So the LORD turned them over to King Jabin of Hazor, a Canaanite king. The commander of his army was Sisera, who lived in Harosheth-haggoyim. ³Sisera, who had 900 iron chariots, ruthlessly oppressed the Israelites for twenty years. Then the people of Israel cried out to the LORD for help.

⁴Deborah, the wife of Lappidoth, was a prophet who was judging Israel at that time. ⁵She would sit under the Palm of Deborah, between Ramah and Bethel in the hill country of Ephraim, and the Israelites would go to her for judgment. ⁶One day she sent for Barak son of Abinoam, who lived in Kedesh in the land of Naphtali. She said to him, "This is what the LORD, the God of Israel, commands you: Call out 10,000 warriors from the tribes of Naphtali and Zebulun at Mount Tabor. ⁷And I will call out Sisera, commander of Jabin's army, along with his chariots and warriors, to the Kishon River. There I will give you victory over him."

⁸Barak told her, "I will go, but only if you go with me."

⁹"Very well," she replied, "I will go with you. But you will receive no honor in this venture, for the LORD's victory over Sisera will be at the hands of a woman." So Deborah went with Barak to Kedesh. ¹⁰At Kedesh, Barak called together the tribes of Zebulun and Naphtali, and 10,000 warriors went up with him. Deborah also went with him.

(Judges 4:1-10)

Reflect

This week's focus is another unlikely heroine. At a time when women held little value by the world's standards, this woman was used by God in mighty ways. Her name is Deborah. Let's backtrack to get to her role in history.

When Moses led the people out of slavery in Egypt, he did just that—he led them. Militarily, spiritually, and politically, Moses was their leader. After him, Joshua led in much the same way but with more emphasis on military conquests. Under Joshua's leadership the people of God were able to conquer and settle into parts of the land promised long ago to Abraham for the Hebrew people. Joshua leaned on the Lord for his direction, and God showed Israel great favor during this time. In Judges 2:7 we read, "And the Israelites served the Lord throughout the lifetime of Joshua and the leaders who outlived him." But just three verses later we read:

> ¹⁰*After that generation died, another generation grew up who did not acknowledge the* Lord *or remember the mighty things he had done for Israel.*
> ¹¹*The Israelites did evil in the* Lord's *sight and served the images of Baal.* ¹²*They abandoned the* Lord, *the God of their ancestors, who had brought them out of Egypt.*
>
> (*Judges 2:10-12a*)

That is one of the saddest passages to me. In just one generation, God's people abandoned their love for Him and grew to be disobedient to the standards set in place by God through Moses. As a result, God allowed them to be plundered. He sold them into the hands of their enemies. His favor no longer rested upon them, and as verse 15 says, "The people were in great distress."

So the Lord raised up new leaders or judges—people very much like Moses and Joshua—who would each lead the nation faithfully as a spiritual, political, and military leader. For a while, under the leadership of each righteous judge, the nation would prosper; but at the death of that person, they would fall back into their evil practices. Again they would find themselves in great distress. The Book of Judges reads like a vicious cycle. "Again the Israelites did evil in the eyes of the Lord" (13:1) is a common phrase. Their disobedience would be followed by God allowing them to fall into the hands of their enemies. The people would repent and cry out to God, and He would raise up a judge to lead them back to Him. Again and again this happened. In fact, in the Book of Judges we see twelve different leaders guide the people of God from prodigal to penitent to prosperous. But with each cycle we see the nation in a downward spiral, straying further and further with each departure from God's standards.

The Book of Judges is dedicated to telling the story of these leaders and the rise and fall of Israel. These leaders were Othniel, Ehud, Shamgar, Deborah, Gideon, Tola, Jair, Jephthah, Ibzan, Elon, Abdon, and Samson. In the books of 1 and 2 Samuel we see the last two judges of Israel, Eli and Samuel. Now, you've most likely heard of Gideon, Deborah, Samuel, and Samson. Jair, Ehud, and Elon, on the other hand, are a little lesser known. For our study this week we will focus on the lone woman in this company—Deborah.

Like Shiphrah and Puah, whom we studied last week, we don't know very much about Deborah either. Was she a mother? No children are mentioned. Was she perhaps named for Rebekah's nursemaid (Genesis 35:8)? No clues are given. How did she grow up? We don't know. There are so many details left untold. Wouldn't you love to know her backstory— who her influencers were, how she came to be regarded so highly by the people of Israel (so much so that they would respect her and travel from afar to have her settle their issues), who her critics were and how she handled them.

Let's recap what we do know about Deborah's life. She was married to a man named Lappidoth. They lived in the hill country of Ephraim, which is located to the west of the Jordan in the mountains that run north to south as you head to the Mediterranean Sea. She would hold court, perhaps much the way that Moses did, to hear the people's concerns and make righteous decisions. She did this under a palm tree that came to be known as the Palm of Deborah. The entire nation would look to her to settle their disputes.

In Judges 4:4-5 we read:

> Israel's leader at that time, the one who was responsible for bringing the people
> back to God, was Deborah, a prophetess, the wife of Lappidoth. She held court
> at a place now called "Deborah's Palm Tree," between Ramah and Bethel,
> in the hill country of Ephraim; and the Israelites came to her to decide their
> disputes. (TLB)

I enjoy these verses in The Living Bible because it tells us that this woman, this righteous judge, was the one responsible for bringing the people back to God. Wow! What a task. How did this come about? Again, we don't have answers to this question. But we do know that Deborah was faithful. At a time when Israel again did evil in the sight of the Lord, she was willing to take a stand. The people must have recognized that God's favor was upon her, for they heeded her advice and allowed her to lead them. Not only did she mediate their disputes but she also led them spiritually and militarily.

With this recap of Deborah's life, let's focus on today's passage. We read that after Ehud's death, the Hebrew nation returned to their evil practices, and as a result they have been ruthlessly oppressed for twenty years by the Canaanites. Under the leadership of King Jabin and the commander of his army, Sisera, the people have suffered greatly. In their distress they remember who had saved them in the past and they cry out to God.

Reread Judges 4:1-10 (page 43). When have you cried out to God in distress?

Recall a time in your life when you strayed from God. What brought you back?

Who has offered godly guidance in your life in the way that Deborah did for the Israelites?

We all need people around us to help keep our compass pointed toward True North. It is so easy to become distracted with the busyness of life, our own agendas, or even sin. When that happens, we can easily spend months—or even years—headed in the wrong direction. Then one day we wake up to a life filled with strife and wonder, *God where are You?* The cycle that is repeated in Judges is one that we can fall into as well.

For instance, we may enjoy a time of walking closely with the Lord. There is an intimacy and sweetness to this season. We may even experience God's blessings. But then life happens and sometimes we drift. Like a boat that isn't securely tied down, we drift farther and farther from shore and find ourselves lost if we don't remain fully rooted in Christ.

"Yes, I am the vine; you are the branches. Those who remain in me, and I in them, will produce much fruit. For apart from me you can do nothing."

(John 15:5)

What season are you in now? Are you enjoying a sweet season of walking closely with Christ, or are you adrift?

So we must listen very carefully to the truth we have heard, or we may drift away from it.

(Hebrews 2:1)

Read John 15:5 in the margin. What is required to bear much fruit and live productively as followers of Christ?

Come close to God, and God will come close to you. Wash your hands, you sinners; purify your hearts, for your loyalty is divided between God and the world.

(James 4:8)

Now read Hebrews 2:1 and James 4:8 in the margin. What can keep us from drifting—or help us once we have drifted—from God's presence?

If you are drifting, simply return to God. He loves you and cares about the hurts and wounds you carry. And He can forgive you for whatever you have done. James 4:8 (NIV) tells us that if we draw near to God, He will draw near to us. That's precious. This is a promise that if we intentionally seek to rekindle a relationship with God, He *will* meet us there. In fact, it may be that you are in a place to call out to God for the first time to establish a real and personal relationship with Him right now. If so, let these Scriptures guide you in that process, and at the close of today's devotional lesson I'll lead you in a prayer that you may pray to give or recommit your life to Jesus.

You will seek me and find me when you seek me with all your heart.

(Jeremiah 29:13 NIV)

Believe in the Lord Jesus and you will be saved, along with everyone in your household.

(Acts 16:31)

For God so loved the world that he gave his one and only Son, that whoever . believes in him shall not perish but have eternal life.

(John 3:16 NIV)

Part of the process of being made right with God is repentance—the choice to turn away from the sin that has separated us from God. Israel needed to repent for falling away from God repeatedly, and so do we. First John 1:9 (NIV) instructs us to confess our sins, promising that "he is faithful and just and will forgive us our sins and purify us from all unrighteousness." This is another precious promise of God's deep and abiding love.

Tomorrow we will see that as the people of God cry out to Him, He honors their request. He gives Deborah, their faithful leader, instructions in how to defeat their overwhelming enemy after two decades of oppression. We, too, can call out to God. Whatever hurts and struggles you are carrying, call out to Him, seeking Him with your whole heart; and as you do, He promises you will find Him with arms outstretched, waiting to hold you.

Pray

- Pray the following prayer, or craft your own prayer to receive Christ or rededicate your life to Him:

Heavenly Father, wash me clean. Forgive me for the ways I have strayed from You in thought and action. I receive Jesus as my Lord and Savior (or recommit my life to Him). Help me to live in ways that please You—to put Your agenda before my own, Your standards in place of the world's, Your love in place of my inadequacies. Help me to love You and those around me in ways that make this world a better place. I love You, God. Help me to love You more. Amen.

DAY 2

Settle

As you tune out today's distractions, consider how God has been at work in your life recently. Thank Him for His presence in your daily activities, and then give Him your full attention as you dive into His Word.

Focus

⁶One day she [Deborah] sent for Barak son of Abinoam, who lived in Kedesh in the land of Naphtali. She said to him, "This is what the LORD, the God of Israel, commands you: Call out 10,000 warriors from the tribes of Naphtali and Zebulun at Mount Tabor. ⁷And I will call out Sisera, commander of Jabin's army, along with his chariots and warriors, to the Kishon River. There I will give you victory over him."

⁸Barak told her, "I will go, but only if you go with me."

⁹. . . So Deborah went with Barak to Kedesh. ¹⁰At Kedesh, Barak called together the tribes of Zebulun and Naphtali, and 10,000 warriors went up with him. Deborah also went with him.

¹¹Now Heber the Kenite, a descendant of Moses' brother-in-law Hobab, had moved away from the other members of his tribe and pitched his tent by the oak of Zaanannim near Kedesh.

¹²When Sisera was told that Barak son of Abinoam had gone up to Mount Tabor, ¹³he called for all 900 of his iron chariots and all of his warriors, and they marched from Harosheth-haggoyim to the Kishon River.

¹⁴Then Deborah said to Barak, "Get ready! This is the day the LORD will give you victory over Sisera, for the LORD is marching ahead of you." So Barak led his 10,000 warriors down the slopes of Mount Tabor into battle. ¹⁵When Barak attacked, the LORD threw Sisera and all his chariots and warriors into a panic. Sisera leaped down from his chariot and escaped on foot. ¹⁶Then Barak chased the chariots and the enemy army all the way to Harosheth-haggoyim, killing all of Sisera's warriors. Not a single one was left alive.

(Judges 4:6-16)

*"And everyone assembled here will know that the L*ORD* rescues his people, but not with sword and spear. This is the L*ORD'*s battle, and he will give you to us!"*

(1 Samuel 17:47)

Reflect

Years ago I struck up a conversation with one of our church greeters. She was a small lady, barely over five feet tall and about 125 pounds, probably in her early sixties. She looked like a spunky, fun grandma. After asking her to share with me some of her story, I learned that this little grandma was more than she appeared. She was a colonel in the United States Air Force, and her specialty was war strategy. She commuted to the Pentagon weekly and met with "people at the top" to discuss best scenarios.

We met in 2002, a time when her gifts were especially important in the aftermath of 9/11. As I got to know her I learned that beyond just shaking people's hands and welcoming them into church service, she was a fierce warrior beneath the kind exterior; a strategic and intelligent woman of God. She reminded me of Deborah. She commanded respect without ever asking for it. Her presence brought wisdom and calm into difficult situations. Yet these gifts were so unexpected; they did not seem to match her appearance. Again, she reminded me of Deborah.

It is not unheard of to find women like my friend in high-ranking positions of authority in business, politics, and even in the military. But around the time of Deborah, this was unprecedented. Deborah is unique as both a spiritual and military leader in Scripture. And she wore this mantle well.

After twenty years of oppression from the Canaanites, the people of God cried out to Him for help. As they turned from their wickedness and again sought the Lord, God answered their prayers and led them through Deborah. She had already earned their trust as a judge, mediating their disputes, and now she brought them God's instructions for how to conquer their enemy.

Wisely, Deborah partnered with Barak, a soldier from northern Israel, where the battle took place. She shared with Barak God's plan, not hers. She told him to gather ten thousand men from the northern tribes of Naphtali and Zebulun and assemble them at Mount Tabor to prepare for battle. Then she lured the armies of Sisera, under the leadership of King Jabin, to the Kishon River valley as God had instructed.

Now picture this, Mount Tabor, though a small mountain, is obviously high ground. It is located to the northwest of the Kishon River. The men of the northern tribes assembled there as Deborah enticed the enemy army into a low-lying dry wadi, or riverbed, of the Kishon River. As Barak's army advanced, the Lord intervened and made this an easy victory for the Israelites.

Read Judges 5, known as "the song of Deborah." Notice especially verses 4 and 21. How was this battle won?

"And everyone assembled here will know that the LORD rescues his people, but not with sword and spear. This is the LORD's battle."
(1 Samuel 17:47)

Now read 1 Samuel 17:47 in the margin. How is this verse similar to Deborah's song?

Though 1 Samuel 17:47 was written about a different circumstance, its truth applies in Deborah's situation also. How does it apply in your own life circumstances?

A wadi is a dry riverbed that is navigable as a path, except in times of rainfall, when it becomes a dangerous channel of water and can even experience flash flooding. Now imagine those nine hundred iron chariots caught in one of the Kishon River wadis as God sent the rain. God's people could not have anticipated how their enemy would be defeated, but they trusted that the battle belonged to the Lord; and they advanced in faith.

There are times in your life when you experience painful consequences, as Israel did, due to your choice of disobedience. In those cases, what is required is repentance and returning to a life that honors God by following His instruction manual, the Bible. But at other times, life happens and you face battles through no fault of your own. In both cases, cry out to God and trust Him to lead you—even when the way is unclear.

Many times in my years of ministry, the way forward has not seemed clear. Who, what, when, where, and how to proceed have been fuzzy. Whenever this happens, I remind myself that the battle belongs to the Lord. Our role is to cry out to Him and then trust and obey as He leads us. In all of our struggles we must remember this verse from 1 Samuel: "This is the LORD's battle" (v. 47).

Deborah was a fierce follower of God. She was relentless in wanting to honor Him and to see His will done in her life and in her nation. This alone is what qualified her to do the job that no other women before her had held in the history of God's people. Long before other warrior women of God such as Joan of Arc, Deborah was leading in unexpected ways. She was an unlikely war strategist, just like my greeter friend.

As a woman in ministry, I've received my share of criticism over the years. After the "spankings" I received from God (see Week 1, Day 2), God began to speak to me through many verses about how He could use me as well as other people who don't fit conventional molds of ministry—people of all kinds of backgrounds.

Read Isaiah 55:8 in the margin. What biblical examples can you think of that illustrate this verse?

"My thoughts are nothing like your thoughts," says the LORD.

"And my ways are far beyond anything you could imagine."
(Isaiah 55:8)

What examples from your own life illustrate the truth of this verse?

Now read 1 Samuel 16:7 in the margin. This was written about King David, but consider how it applies today—generally and to your own life. Jot down your thoughts below:

Deborah not only led as a woman of God; she led successfully. God gave her victory in battle as she followed His instructions closely. Tomorrow we will consider the character traits we see her display and how we, too, can find success as we fight the battles that are before us. What battles are you fighting? Perhaps it is a struggle to see the salvation of a loved one, a battle against addiction, a war against injustice, a battle to restore your marriage or fight against a disease. Whatever it is, remember that these battles belong to the Lord. Trust Him to fight for you as you follow Him closely.

I saw a funny T-shirt recently that said "Underestimate Me—That ought to be fun!" Deborah, Shiphrah, Puah, and the other women we are examining in our study could all be models for this slogan. But perhaps the One who really displays this is God Himself. So often we become trapped in wondering if we are able. Can we handle it? The real question should be "Is our God able?" And that answer is *yes*! God chooses to use unexpected people in unexpected ways to accomplish His will. We need only be fiercely available and obedient.

Pray

- Pray the following prayer, or craft your own prayer acknowledging that your battles belong to the Lord and asking Him to help you as you wait to see the victory:

Almighty God, I know that You are able! You are able to fight the battles I face and emerge as Victor. In fact, the victory is already Yours! Help me to stay close to You. Draw me into Your presence, and help me understand the path that lays before me. Give me patience, peace, and strength in the waiting periods.

(Name your specific battles now and ask God for His guidance as you seek His will.)

Thank You, Lord, that You are able and that I can stand behind Your shield in the battles of my life. Thank you! Thank You! Amen.

DAY 3

Settle

Take the time to sing a song to the Lord, perhaps a favorite hymn or childhood song that brings you comfort. Remember, we are told to make a joyful noise to the Lord: "Make a joyful noise unto the LORD, all ye lands. / Serve the LORD with gladness: come before his presence with singing" (Psalm 100:1-2 KJV). God doesn't care about how talented your singing is; just sing to Him with joy!

Focus

²²But the fruit of the Spirit is love, joy, peace, forbearance, kindness, goodness, faithfulness, ²³gentleness and self-control.

(Galatians 5:22-23a NIV)

²⁹"Many women do noble things,
    but you surpass them all."
³⁰Charm is deceptive, and beauty is fleeting;
    but a woman who fears the LORD is to be praised.

(Proverbs 31:29-30 NIV)

Reflect

OK, if I'm being honest, I've always been a firecracker. I'm one of those feisty girls who is ready for an adventure and a challenge. Just sitting still always seemed like such a waste of time to me. As a child, my mom would have my brothers and me take an hour after lunch for reading and reflection. It was brutal! There were things to do, places to go, adventures to be had!

That spirit of adventure has taken me on some amazing journeys in my life. But again, if I'm being honest, that feisty attitude toward life also gets me into trouble every now and then. So as a young adult I decided I needed to be more like a graceful Southern lady. I would be gentle, reserved, and quiet. Isn't that what a woman of God is supposed to be?

Let me explain. I grew up in the South—the Deep South, where real Southern belles drop their r's and elongate their syllables. I grew up as

Janefa (not Jennifer) from the state of Joja (not Georgia). Say it out loud and you'll get it.

There was a lady in our church who exemplified Southern grace to me. Perhaps you've known someone like this. She probably has embossed stationery. She sits with her ankles crossed. She speaks gently, carries herself well, and still wears slips. Do you know this lady? She's refined, graceful, and dignified. She was and still is a heroine in my life. So, I tried for a while to be like her. I bought the slip and the stationery. (My husband thought it was hysterical.)

Problem was, it wasn't working for me. It was not authentic to who I am deep inside. You'll remember from last week, I'm the girl who brought the Ex-Lax cookies. I also am the girl who accidentally started a college-wide food fight, but that's another story. Anyway, feisty runs through my veins. It took me a few years to figure out that instead of becoming this other person, I just needed to become who God had designed me to be from the beginning. A firecracker, with less Ex-Lax and fewer food fights.

I began a quest to discover how my personality, a feisty one, could be used for God's purposes in fierce and significant ways. Now, I'm still figuring this out, and somedays feisty outweighs fierce, but through my graceful Southern lady experiment I began to search the Scriptures to discover exactly what kind of character I was really trying to achieve.

Several Scriptures became my guideposts. First, there was the passage on the fruit of the Spirit in Galatians 5, and then Proverbs 31, which describes a hardworking, loyal, godly, and fierce woman of God.

Read Galatians 5:13-26. What does Paul warn against in these verses?

What attributes or fruit does Paul say will be evident in the life of someone controlled by God's Spirit?

What areas do you need to surrender to God's control?

Now read through Proverbs 31:10-31. How might we describe the depiction of a virtuous woman today?

We each have to discover how God has created us and learn to work with those attributes. Are you creative, intellectual, crafty, compassionate, winsome, or strategic? These are qualities that God placed within you, and He wants us to use them to achieve His goals. But sometimes we focus on our shortcomings, even seeing what could be an attribute—such as feistiness—as a negative. We have to learn to become comfortable with how God has created us in order to fully reach the potential God has placed inside us.

My version of a fierce woman of God was not supposed to look like the woman in my church I so revered. She, in her own way, was fierce. But my version would look slightly different. And that, I learned, was OK. In fact, it was great. Because God creates us all uniquely.

Fierce women of God come in many shapes and sizes. They have different interests, personalities, talents, and giftings. But there are some traits that mature women of God share—they are faithful, patient, wise, kind, humble, and just. Fierce women of God put a face to the Scriptures you have just read from Proverbs and Galatians. Their lives bear evidence of the fruit of the Spirit and exemplify the qualities of the virtuous woman outlined in Proverbs 31.

Deborah was one of these women—a fierce woman of God. Surely she knew that she did not fit the traditional roles women played in her lifetime. She was an unlikely heroine whom God used at a time when Israel needed a leader. As we examine her life, we see five attributes that served her well. No matter the personality type or interests, these characteristics are common to all women whom God uses in mighty ways. So, it will serve us well if we seek them also. Let's consider them together.

1. Wisdom. Daily Deborah sat under the palm tree to settle disputes among God's people (Judges 4:5). She was trusted to impart wisdom in fair and just ways. Obviously, she had demonstrated wisdom in her judgments. Deborah depended on God to lead her as she led others.

Where do you need to seek God's wisdom in your own life?

2. Righteousness. By definition, righteousness is a state of living morally justified. I like to think of it as "right living." The people would have been reluctant to follow Deborah if they thought she did not personally live by God's standards.

What in your life needs attention for you to live with moral purity and above the reproach of others?

3. Humility. As Deborah carried out God's instructions, she was careful to give Him the credit. In fact, all of Judges 5 is a song where Deborah and Barak give God the credit and praise for the victory.

Does it matter to you who gets the credit for your successes? How has humility, or the lack of it, impacted your service to the Lord?

4. Strength. Imagine the criticism Deborah must have endured as the lone female leader of the nation. If Moses endured the Israelites' grumbling, just imagine what Deborah experienced! Clearly she possessed great strength of character, resulting from her relationship with God. Lack of strength stops many women from reaching their full potential.

How is God calling you to "toughen up" in and through Him so that you may be strong for Him?

5. Obedience. Hearing God speak and acting on what He tells us are two very different things. Deborah had the courage and conviction to do both. She heard from the Lord and she put into motion His will.

What helps you to follow God closely?

What keeps you from following God closely?

Deborah's qualifications for leadership were her character and her calling. And that is enough by God's standards. When we maintain godly character and lean into the calling God has placed on our lives, we are able to partner with Him to do fierce things!

Deborah plays a unique role in biblical history because she brought godly character and what I like to think was a feisty personality under God's control. As you seek to live as a fierce woman of God, remember that God is not calling you to be like anyone else. You carry your own unique giftings, personality, and passions. Allow God to shape these so that you can be used mightily to make this world a more Christlike planet.

Pray

- Take time to thank God for some of your unique qualities.
- Ask Him how He might want to use these qualities to bless others and bring glory to Himself.
- As you pray, listen to "Fearfully and Wonderfully Made," written and recorded by Matt Redman (or another relevant song of your choice).

DAY 4

Settle

Perhaps you know the old hymn "What a Friend We Have in Jesus," written by Joseph M. Scriven. Review these lyrics as you begin your devotional time today:

> What a Friend we have in Jesus,
>   All our sins and griefs to bear!
> What a privilege to carry
>   Everything to God in prayer!
>
> O what peace we often forfeit,
>   O what needless pain we bear,
> All because we do not carry
>   Everything to God in prayer!

Focus

[28]Then Jesus said, "Come to me, all of you who are weary and carry heavy burdens, and I will give you rest. [29]Take my yoke upon you. Let me teach you, because I am humble and gentle at heart, and you will find rest for your souls. [30]For my yoke is easy to bear, and the burden I give you is light."

(Matthew 11:28-30)

But seek first his kingdom and his righteousness, and all these things will be given to you as well.

(Matthew 6:33 NIV)

Reflect

How many hats do you wear in a typical week? Working woman, volunteer, ministry leader, daughter, friend, sister, wife, mom—the list can go on and on. And it can become exhausting, can't it?

When my kids were ages five and one, my husband and I moved to a new area to launch a church. It was an exciting time, but wow was it consuming! I was teaching fitness classes and trying to make new friends, establish the kids in new routines, spend time with family who lived hours away, stay connected with old friends, and work forty-plus hours a week in order to help get this new ministry off the ground. I was tired, and probably a little grumpy.

Getting up at 3:30 am in order to "get things done" became a regular practice for a while, but it was taking a toll. I would switch hats every few minutes, trying to balance all of these responsibilities. But everything was suffering: my marriage, my kids, my attitude, and my relationship with God. Even my relationship with myself was struggling. It was simply too many hats to wear.

Can you relate to this struggle? For many of us, the to-do list seems endless. We become consumed with the urgent, others' expectations, and even our own expectations; and life becomes overwhelming. We live in a perpetual state of fatigue and mediocrity.

As I journeyed through this season, I often complained to my mom, my husband, and even God. I guess I expected them to step in and solve it for me. But after two years of whining and exhaustion, I was at a physical and emotional breaking point. So, I went to see a counselor.

When have you experienced a time of exhaustion and fatigue?

During this difficult time, what was your relationship with Christ like?

The counselor I saw was a Christian and a no-nonsense kind of person who listened for a while and then looked at me and said, "Well, it sounds like you have a pride issue." I was offended. I was drowning in the responsibilities of my life, depressed, and scared, and he had the audacity to add one more struggle to this list. Pride!

He went on to explain that he felt it was pride, at least in part, that was keeping me from letting go of some of my responsibilities. Pride was the reason I was working so hard. Pride had kept me from handing off tasks and simplifying my life.

But my counselor wasn't done with his tough love. Apparently, fear was an issue too. Great, something else. But this one I understood immediately. I was working hard for long hours because I was afraid of failing. I didn't want to let God down. I didn't want to disappoint my husband or kids. I was afraid of rejection in establishing new relationships. I didn't want to be a failure. Fear and pride—they're often intertwined.

Wow! It was an aha moment for me. The source of my pain was unrecognized sin in my life.

I had wanted to blame my husband and kids for expecting so much—or the people of the church for being so needy. But my real source of pain was coming from my own sinful nature.

I don't remember all that the counselor said, but I do remember that through this process I began to live for an Audience of One. I had to let go of the expectations that I and others had and instead focus on what God was speaking into my life. I had to repent of seeking after my own definition of success and focus solely on God's. It was a defining moment for me.

Now, the needs of my family and church were real and continue to be present, but I've found that this is manageable when I have my life in order. Have you noticed that when you have inner peace there is no outer chaos that can unravel you?

Through this journey as a young adult I focused on what matters most. What will I regret twenty years from now? I became committed to living with intentionality. As a wife, mom, ministry leader, daughter, and friend, how should I spend my time? It gave me permission to let some stuff go and emphasized the need to become tenacious in other areas. It determined what I said yes to, but perhaps even more important, it determined when I said no.

For instance, I always wanted to encourage my kids to do their best in academics and sports. If that went well, great; if not, no huge problem. On the other hand, when it came to character, those issues were deal breakers. Being honest, having integrity, showing compassion, displaying kindness, keeping a promise, reflecting a good work ethic, studying God's Word—these were areas that were nonnegotiable in our household. If that meant less time on homework and they got a B, it was OK. But lying—that was never OK!

God made Himself very real to me during this time of searching and helped to establish guidelines for how to live my life well and set expectations. It taught me about healthy balance and priorities.

One of the women in my life who exemplifies balance really well is my next-door neighbor. She owns and operates a large and thriving business. She's married, a fitness enthusiast, and a foster parent. Oh, and did I mention she also has six kids! But what sticks out most upon meeting her is that she loves Jesus! Her entire life is a rotating-hat circus act, but she pulls it off with grace and success because she has created a healthy rhythm in her life. She has put in the effort to become very intentional in how she organizes her time. While the kids are in school, she makes time to be with God, train her staff, meet with clients, exercise, have lunch with friends, and volunteer in ministries that she is passionate about. And when she's with you, she's present—not distracted with what's next but fully present in the moment. That's rare and precious. As I have watched my neighbor live out her crazy, busy, and fun life, I've seen that what holds it all together is her center. At the center of all she does is her love for Christ, her Audience of One.

For most of us women, life is a juggling act. And sometimes it feels like we are dropping all the balls, doesn't it? How do we find a rhythm that is healthy? By finding our identity in Christ and allowing His expectations to become our own.

Do you feel you have a healthy, productive rhythm in your life at this point? What feels right and healthy? What feels burdensome or out of balance?

Make a list of what consumes your daily life:

Read Matthew 11:28-30 in the margin. Does the burden you are carrying feel light? Could it be that you are carrying a yoke that God never intended for you to bear?

How can Matthew 6:33 (in the margin) help guide your time—your thoughts and actions?

God promises us that the weight He intends for us to carry is not only manageable but also light. So if your load is heavy, as mine was during the dark time I shared, perhaps you are carrying a load God never intended for you to have.

Pray over your list of things that consume your daily life (page 64), and ask God to reveal any areas that He wants you to focus on and any He wants you to cut back on or even eliminate. Draw a star beside those God wants you to focus on; draw an X beside those He wants you to cut back on or eliminate.

Surely Deborah, the fierce woman of the Bible we are studying this week, wore many hats. We know that she was a wife, a war strategist, a prophetess, a judge and mediator, and a guide for an entire nation. These are no small roles. But we've also seen that Deborah knew when to seek the help of others in order to balance the responsibilities of her life. She summoned Barak as her army general, and through his leadership the northern tribes were assembled and prepared for battle. Because she stayed close to the Lord, not allowing fear and pride to skew her leadership, she followed God's directions closely and gave Him the praise for all success. This was the key to how she juggled her responsibilities—with humility and faithfulness.

God wants us to lead in much the same way, laying aside our will to embrace His. Through that type of surrendered attitude God is able to use and bless us in extraordinary ways!

28Then Jesus said, "Come to me, all of you who are weary and carry heavy burdens, and I will give you rest. 29Take my yoke upon you. Let me teach you, because I am humble and gentle at heart, and you will find rest for your souls. 30For my yoke is easy to bear, and the burden I give you is light."
(Matthew 11:28-30)

Seek the Kingdom of God above all else, and live righteously, and he will give you everything you need.
(Matthew 6:33)

Pray

- Consider again the old hymn "What a Friend We Have in Jesus." You may want to sing or hum it to God prayerfully, asking Him to reveal to you where you are forfeiting peace by carrying a weight alone.
- Ask God to guide you in managing your list of responsibilities. What would He have you release?
- Thank God for His access to you as a friend.

DAY 5

Settle

Put aside today's to-do list for a moment and be still. Once your heart is settled, pray to God:

> ¹*Let all that I am praise the* LORD;
>> *with my whole heart, I will praise his holy name.*
> ²*Let all that I am praise the* LORD;
>> *may I never forget the good things he does for me.*
>
> (Psalm 103:1-2)

Focus

¹*On that day Deborah and Barak son of Abinoam sang this song:*

> ²*"When the princes in Israel take the lead,*
>> *when the people willingly offer themselves—*
>> *praise the* LORD!
> ³*"Hear this, you kings! Listen, you rulers!*
>> *I, even I, will sing to the* LORD;
>> *I will praise the* LORD, *the God of Israel, in song."*
>
> (Judges 5:1-3 NIV)

⁹*"This, then, is how you should pray:*

> '*Our Father in heaven,*
> *hallowed be your name,*
> ¹⁰*your kingdom come,*
> *your will be done,*
>> *on earth as it is in heaven.*
> ¹¹*Give us today our daily bread.*
> ¹²*And forgive us our debts,*
>> *as we also have forgiven our debtors.'*"
>
> (Matthew 6:9-12 NIV)

³⁹*Jesus went out as usual to the Mount of Olives, and his disciples followed him.* ⁴⁰*On reaching the place, he said to them, "Pray that you will not fall*

into temptation." [41]*He withdrew about a stone's throw beyond them, knelt down and prayed,* [42]*"Father, if you are willing, take this cup from me; yet not my will, but yours be done."*

(*Luke* 22:39-42 NIV)

Reflect

One of my dearest friends has a job that few women occupy. She is a commercial airline pilot. In her company only a small percentage of the more than fourteen thousand pilots are female, making her part of a distinct minority in her field. As a woman serving in a position traditionally held by men, she has, not too surprisingly, faced challenges from time to time.

There are the passengers who regularly ask her to hang up their coats or get them some coffee, which she does gladly. There are those who seem nervous to fly with a woman at the controls and even thank her with surprise when they exit the plane after a smooth landing. And surely she has felt the loneliness of travel in a profession where there are so few female colleagues.

She also has felt the challenge of juggling the various roles in her life. My friend is one of those women who wears many hats. She is a wife, daughter, follower of Christ, friend, and mother of three beautiful girls—two of whom have significant special needs.

But she loves flying. She's a great pilot and a born leader. It's how God wired her. So she has learned to balance her strength and leadership with grace and humility. Can a woman be strong, lead well, and still be a feminine creation of God? Yes! Absolutely! But notice that strength must be balanced with humility and grace. This is essential to obtain a healthy and pleasing balance in the life of a godly woman.

When my friend was telling me about hanging up the coats and getting the coffee, I thought she would be aggravated, maybe even a bit insulted. After all, she has worked hard and long to get to this position of leadership. But instead she said, "I just do what is asked as long as it doesn't interfere with my main role as the pilot." She finds no need to correct or redirect these passengers. There's no need to point out that they've made an erroneous assumption. She just serves them.

This is humble leadership.

Do you know a woman who exhibits humble leadership like my friend? If so, describe her briefly:

My friend strives to live her life under God's control, and that allows her to be confident, strong, humble, and filled with peace. Strength under the Holy Spirit's direction looks good on Christ followers. It allows us to be strong and to serve, lead well, and still show kindness. A woman who has surrendered her heart, attitudes, and actions to God can live with a fierce sense of purpose, unconcerned with what others think or what roles they think they are supposed to fit into.

Now, you may be thinking, "Well, I'm not really a leader, so this doesn't apply to me." But think about it: we all are leaders in some arenas. It may be that you lead a large company, a classroom, a dance class, your children, or a friend group. Leadership is influence; and whether we realize it or not, we all have opportunities to lead on a daily basis.

Leading with strength can be a struggle for us as women trying to follow God closely and be effective in ministry. In wanting to make a difference in the world, we sometimes feel the tension of being both gentle and decisive, feminine and fierce. We don't want to be labeled as too aggressive, but we do want to get things done. Can the two truly coexist?

Let's consider Deborah again. She certainly did not fit the stereotypes of her time. Like my friend, she was in the distinct minority in her role as a military, political, and religious leader. Yet she led with strength and wisdom. She sought the help of others and gave them credit for their contributions. Her directions were clear and strong, but they came straight from the Lord; so when the battle was completed, it was to God alone that she sang her praises.

Read the victory song of Deborah found in Judges 5. How does she praise God for what has been accomplished? To whom else does she give credit?

It is a sign of maturity and humility to be able to celebrate the successes of others the way Deborah does with Jael and Barak in Judges 5. How can you help others celebrate the victories in their lives?

In your victories and accomplishments, how can you privately and publicly give God the glory?

As we consider the qualities of a heroic and fierce woman of God, we see several common characteristics:

- Her identity is wrapped up in her relationship with Christ.
- She values God's opinion over the opinion of those around her.
- A fierce woman of God is passionate about living with purpose.
- She is filled with gratitude for who God created her to be.
- She is an encourager of others.
- Her character is strong and bold, yet kind and gentle.
- She protects those who cannot protect themselves.
- She has the power to influence others because she lives under the control of the Holy Spirit.
- The fierce woman of God seeks not her own will but God's will to be done in her life.
- Others recognize Christ at work in her.
- Though she is not perfect, she strives for holiness in all she does.

What characteristics would you add to this list?

Reread Matthew 6:9-12. Now rewrite this as your personal prayer to God below, giving special attention to the phrases about God's kingdom coming and God's will being done:

Now, consider our last passage from today's Focus readings, where we find Jesus in the garden of Gethsemane. Jesus knew that His time for the cross had come. Imagine the inner turmoil He must have been experiencing. The Man who healed the blind and calmed the sea could have called down angels from heaven and put an end to this misery. But instead He prayed, "Yet not my will, but yours be done" (v. 42).

Reread Luke 22:39-42 (pages 67–68). (You may want to read the entire garden of Gethsemane account in your Bible, which continues through verse 46.) How does this demonstrate heroic leadership?

When have you been torn between your will and God's will? How did you respond?

Though it's a pale comparison, Jesus surrendering to God's will is like my friend getting the coffee and Deborah leading the army of God: Jesus put aside His own desires to serve others. Some would call this weakness, but we know better. This is true strength. It is heroic leadership. When someone in power puts aside their own agenda to care for those who can't or won't care for themselves, it is love. And it is what we are called to offer those around us.

In our areas of leadership—however great or small—let's seek to follow the examples we have seen this week. May we lead boldly with kindness and humility that point others to Jesus.

Pray

- Pray the following prayer, or craft your own prayer asking God to help you surrender your will for His:

Dear Jesus, thank You for Your example of how to love others deeply, even sacrificially. Please guide and help me to follow that example by humbly putting aside my will in order to fully embrace Yours. Thank You for the example of Deborah, a woman who was faithful in her lifetime. May the same to be said of me. I love You, Lord. Amen.

Video Viewer Guide: Week 2

*So the L*ORD *turned them over to King Jabin of Hazor, a Canannite king. The commander of his army was Sisera . . . who had 900 iron chariots [and] ruthlessly oppressed the Israelites for twenty years. Then the people of Israel cried out to the L*ORD *for help.*

Deborah, the wife of Lappidoth, was a prophet who was judging Israel at that time. She would sit under the Palm of Deborah, between Ramah and Bethel in the hill country of Ephraim, and the Israelites would go to her for judgement. (Judges 4:2-5)

"Wake up, Deborah, wake up!
Wake up, wake up, and sing a song!"
(Judges 5:12a)

What if's can steal a lot of _____ and _____ in our lives.

*"Blessed is the one who trusts in the L*ORD*,*
whose confidence is in him." (Jeremiah 17:7 NIV)

Our confidence is not in _____; it's in what God can do _____ us if we turn our lives over to Him.

"No eye has seen, no ear has heard,
and no mind has imagined
what God has prepared
for those who love him."
(1 Corinthians 2:9)

We must get rid of our _____.

I can do all things through Christ who strengthens me. (Philippians 4:13 NKJV)

Week 3

Naaman's Slave Girl

2 Kings 5

DAY 1

Settle

Stand up and take a deep breath in, reaching over your head as you hold that breath a few seconds; then slowly exhale. Now try it again. As you breathe in, invite the Holy Spirit to fill you; and as you breathe out, release the stresses that would distract you as you spend time with Jesus today.

Focus

¹The king of Aram had great admiration for Naaman, the commander of his army, because through him the LORD had given Aram great victories. But though Naaman was a mighty warrior, he suffered from leprosy.

²At this time Aramean raiders had invaded the land of Israel, and among their captives was a young girl who had been given to Naaman's wife as a maid. ³One day the girl said to her mistress, "I wish my master would go to see the prophet in Samaria. He would heal him of his leprosy."

⁴So Naaman told the king what the young girl from Israel had said. ⁵"Go and visit the prophet," the king of Aram told him. "I will send a letter of introduction for you to take to the king of Israel." So Naaman started out, carrying as gifts 750 pounds of silver, 150 pounds of gold, and ten sets of clothing. ⁶The letter to the king of Israel said: "With this letter I present my servant Naaman. I want you to heal him of his leprosy."

⁷When the king of Israel read the letter, he tore his clothes in dismay and said, "Am I God, that I can give life and take it away? Why is this man asking me to heal someone with leprosy? I can see that he's just trying to pick a fight with me."

⁸But when Elisha, the man of God, heard that the king of Israel had torn his clothes in dismay, he sent this message to him: "Why are you so upset? Send Naaman to me, and he will learn that there is a true prophet here in Israel."

⁹So Naaman went with his horses and chariots and waited at the door of Elisha's house.

(2 Kings 5:1-9)

Reflect

As we read in 2 Kings, God's people have again been unfaithful to the Lord. No longer is Israel a superpower as they were under the reign of King David. No longer do they enjoy the benefits enjoyed during the time of Solomon. God has allowed enemies to invade because of Israel's unwillingness to serve Him. Among the enemies surrounding Israel is a small country to the northeast called Aram, which is modern-day Syria. During the raids between Israel and her enemies, many Israelites became casualties of war or were captured and sold in the slave markets.

One of these prisoners of war is this week's heroine. Scripture never reveals her name. In fact, very little is written about her at all. There are only two verses dedicated to her, yet from these verses we see great character. She is a child who has been ripped from her parents during a time of war. She has been taken to a new country, a new home—one with a different religion, customs, and expectations. Most likely she was sold at the slave market in Damascus. Humiliated and afraid, she no longer plays in the field around her home; she now serves as a maid to the wife of one of Aram's greatest commanders. Imagine the tears this child has shed.

We also know that this young girl has been raised to know, love, and trust the one true God. We see that despite desperate circumstances she has clung to her faith.

Reread 2 Kings 5:1-3 (page 75). What do you think this little girl must be feeling?

The commander's home in which our young heroine served belonged to Naaman. He was a man who had won great respect for his triumph in battles—specifically from the king of Aram. He was well thought of and held great power. But Naaman had a medical crisis. He had contracted the deadly disease of leprosy, a skin disease that had no cure and was highly contagious. Naaman and his household knew that as the leprosy progressed, the entire family would be at risk and eventually he would become a social outcast. Surely his wife, whom our young heroine served, was distraught over her husband's illness.

This is where our young maiden speaks up and her fierce faith shines through. "I wish my master would go to see the prophet in Samaria. He would heal him of his leprosy," she pleads with her mistress in verse 3. It is this young Israelite who has compassion on her master and offers her best advice: take him to see the prophet of God in Israel, Elisha. She knows that even in a foreign land the power of God is at work, and she is willing to share this with those who have captured her.

As I read this little girl's story, there are several things that shine through; but perhaps, most of all, I am struck with her fierce faith in a difficult situation. She is a child slave. She has been snatched from her home. Sold! Surely at some point she had to ask, "God, where are you? Why haven't you rescued me? Where is my mom? God, don't you care?" Surely, she must have felt angry, sad, scared, and confused. But what we see in this brief encounter is a rock-solid faith in God. This little girl knows that despite her own situation, God is able.

I often sit down to talk with people going through difficult life circumstances. It's interesting how differently people process their setbacks in life. One couple going through a miscarriage, for instance, may be filled with anger toward God, while another is thankful for His presence in their pain. A business owner forced to close up shop may be depressed and confused about whether God even exists, while another in a similar situation may see it as God directing her to new opportunities.

How is it that two people can go through similar situations and come out in such different places?

Largely the outcome is determined by the person's depth of faith and maturity in Christ. This little girl is not caught up in the *Why me?* syndrome that adults so often fall prey to. She holds on to the one constant in her life: her faith in God.

When you experience difficulties in life, how do you typically respond?

How has your relationship with God been impacted in difficult seasons?

Read Matthew 18:2-4 in the margin. What do Jesus' words teach us about faith?

When asked by His disciples, "Who is the greatest in the Kingdom of Heaven?" Jesus responds by inviting a child to come and be with them. This child is the object lesson for the disciples. Jesus holds up this child who, in that culture, had no rights and no voice, and says that the one who takes on the same position—innocent and childlike—is great in the eyes of heaven. Childlike faith is not weak; it is pure and strong.

Our fierce heroine this week is a little girl living and serving as a slave in a foreign country. What an unlikely hero. What a difficult situation in which to shine. But shine she does. As we will see through the week, in just two verses she teaches us about compassion, faith, and courage. She is fierce!

Pray

- Listen to Matt Redman's recording of "Blessed Be Your Name" (or another relevant song of your choice), paying attention to the lyrics about being in a desert place and praising when the darkness closes in.
- Ask God to give you the wisdom to seek Him in your desert places and to praise Him in your suffering.
- Thank God that He is close even in our times of hurt and brokenness.

DAY 2

Settle

If the weather is nice, head outside today. Find a quiet spot and just be still for a few moments, enjoying God's presence in solitude. Or if that's not an option today, find a quiet space inside. Wherever you are, what sounds do you notice?

Focus

¹The king of Aram had great admiration for Naaman, the commander of his army, because through him the LORD had given Aram great victories. But though Naaman was a mighty warrior, he suffered from leprosy.

²At this time Aramean raiders had invaded the land of Israel, and among their captives was a young girl who had been given to Naaman's wife as a maid. ³One day the girl said to her mistress, "I wish my master would go to see the prophet in Samaria. He would heal him of his leprosy."

(2 Kings 5:1-3)

The LORD is close to the brokenhearted
*   and saves those who are crushed in spirit.*

(Psalm 34:18 NIV)

"I have told you these things, so that in me you may have peace. In this world you will have trouble. But take heart! I have overcome the world."

(John 16:33 NIV)

Now faith is confidence in what we hope for and assurance about what we do not see.

(Hebrews 11:1 NIV)

Reflect

My local church is heavily involved in prison ministries. Let me tell you how this came about. A couple of years ago my husband and I were preaching a series on the life of Daniel called "Thriving in Babylon." At the end of the first service, one of our church attenders asked for a video of the service to share at his place of work. Turns out this man was a warden. God had spoken to his heart during the message, and he wanted to see the men he served learn to thrive in their Babylon the way Daniel did.

For several weeks we sent a video of the message to be shared in the prison, and soon the crowd grew from a few dozen to more than a hundred. We engaged as a church and began to get to know the prisoners, pray for them, take Bibles to them, and learn their stories. But we knew sending the video and a staff person weekly would not be enough. As the primary communicators, we knew we had to get to know these men personally.

Let me be honest with you, the idea of going into an all-male prison facility scared me. Going through the metal detector and then hearing the door clang shut behind me is a moment I will never forget. But the blessings I have received in the visits there have changed my life.

On our first visit, several things struck me. When we went into the dorm, the inmates lined up beside their cell doors. Standing at attention, hands behind their backs, we saw boys. These were young men just sixteen and seventeen years old. They looked hard. Their stares were cold and blank until they recognized us from the video; then they silently began to mouth greetings to us and, one by one, break into smiles.

The next dorm we visited was for "lifers," men serving lifetime sentences with no chance of parole. This facility was spotless. They took care of their environment, resigned to the fact that this was their home. These men did not stand at attention; they walked freely about. Upon seeing us, they walked up to me and my husband and greeted us warmly. One man approached my husband with his Bible and asked for an autograph. Now this was a funny moment to me. I thought, *No way— you better not sign that book. God wrote that!* Fortunately, Jim thought the same thing. He said he immediately saw himself standing before God in heaven, hearing, "So, I hear you've been taking credit for my book." Nobody wants to have that conversation! So instead of "autographing" it, he wrote a blessing and Scripture in it.

The next thing that happened really touched me. An older man approached me and said, "Thank you for your messages. I've been in for thirty years. It's time I learned to thrive in my Babylon." Later that night when we attended the service, it was this man who had put out the chairs so that the other inmates wouldn't have to do it themselves, poured drinks for them, and swept up after the service. And he did these things with *joy*. It was my privilege to come alongside him that night and serve those drinks.

I will never forget his words, "It's time I learned to thrive in my Babylon." I thought of people suffering with diseases such as cystic fibrosis, cerebral palsy, and cancer as well as addiction, depression, and bipolar disorder. I thought of friends who were going through unwanted divorce, those who had lost a child or spouse too soon in life, and people going through financial distress—all who felt lonely and perhaps even unloved. These are also our Babylons and, like my newfound friend in the prison, we have to learn to thrive in them.

Sometimes we find ourselves living in Babylon through our own poor decisions. But sometimes life just happens. Disease, financial crises, and broken relationships are, unfortunately, part of the human condition—the result of a world marred by sin and brokenness. It is in these times that we have the choice to turn from God or run to Him. Will we choose to thrive in our Babylon?

What Babylons have you experienced?

Did you survive or thrive during those times? Explain your response.

Read Psalm 34:18 (page 79). How can this verse help you as you travel through dark times?

The Bible shares some amazing stories about children: Isaac, Joseph, Moses, David, and a little slave girl; and this little girl is truly remarkable. Though we don't even know her name, we do know something of her life, as we learned yesterday. Captured in a raid from enemies from the north, she was taken from her home against her will. Perhaps her family had been slaughtered. Now she finds herself serving in the home of a high-ranking military leader of the Aramean army as his wife's handmaid. How long has she been there? Has she been treated well? There are so many things we do not know about her, but today I want to lift up one important thing we do know.

Reread 2 Kings 5:3 (page 79). What wish or hope did she express, and what was her motivation?

This servant girl has compassion on someone suffering and courageously speaks up to offer help. She wants to help her master. Notice that she does not say God might heal him; she says it will happen. This is important. Her faith is so strong that she offers the suggestion to see Elisha, fully believing in advance that Naaman will be healed. That's fierce faith.

What is faith according to Hebrews 11:1 (page 79)?

Read the entire chapter of Hebrews 11 in your Bible, and outline below what happened to each of these biblical heroes and heroines as they moved in faith.

<u>Who</u>   <u>What Happened Through Faith</u>

Abel

Enoch

Noah

Abraham

Who	What Happened Through Faith
Sarah	
Isaac	
Jacob	
Joseph	
Moses' parents	
Moses	
The people of Israel	
Rahab	

Despite the fact that she is living as a slave in a foreign land, this girl demonstrates confident faith in the power of God to work through his prophet Elisha to heal her master's leprosy. In her own distress she has not given up on God. That is a powerful lesson for us. We can have this confidence as well, depending not only on God's power but also on the promises of Jesus.

Reread John 16:33 (page 79), and then read Romans 8:38-39 in the margin. What are the promises contained in these verses?

How have your struggles affected your relationship with God?

[38]And I am convinced that nothing can ever separate us from God's love. Neither death nor life, neither angels nor demons, neither our fears for today nor our worries about tomorrow—not even the powers of hell can separate us from God's love. [39]No power in the sky above or in the earth below—indeed, nothing in all creation will ever be able to separate us from the love of God that is revealed in Christ Jesus our Lord. (Romans 8:38-39)

What testimonies of God's faithfulness during difficult times do you have that could encourage others, and how might you use them?

Who is going through a tough time, like Naaman, whom you could show compassion?

One of the places I've had to muster courage to show compassion and develop real relationships has been in the prisons. And what a blessing—definitely to me, and I hope to them. It has been thrilling to see men begin to thrive in their tough settings. In fact, as the men have been transferred from one facility to another, word has spread that God can change lives within the walls. As a result, our prison ministry has grown rapidly. We are now serving hundreds of inmates weekly in several different facilities, and we always begin with the series "Thriving in Babylon." (And, yes, many more Bibles have been signed with a blessing!)

As God's children, we are not promised that we will not face difficulties, but we are promised that God will be with us. When we learn to thrive through the Babylons of our lives, it is a powerful testimony that needs few words. A woman who comes through the fires of life with gentle strength; a powerful, loving heart; and faithful resolve is truly fierce. Through such women God is changing the world and offering hope to others who are hurting.

Let's face our struggles as the little handmaiden did—fiercely!

Pray

- Cry out to God about the struggles you are facing.
- Ask Him to show you ways you can thrive in these difficulties and even reach out to others in their pain.
- Thank God that He is with the brokenhearted and those who are crushed in spirit.

DAY 3

Settle

Play an old love song such as Elvis's recording of "Love Me Tender" or Bryan Adams's "(Everything I Do) I Do It for You" or another song of your choice, and imagine the lyrics are straight from God to you today.

Focus

¹The king of Syria had high admiration for Naaman, the commander-in-chief of his army, for he had led his troops to many glorious victories. So he was a great hero, but he was a leper. ²Bands of Syrians had invaded the land of Israel, and among their captives was a little girl who had been given to Naaman's wife as a maid.

³One day the little girl said to her mistress, "I wish my master would go to see the prophet in Samaria. He would heal him of his leprosy!"

(2 Kings 5:1-3 TLB)

"My grace is all you need, for my power is greatest when you are weak."

(2 Corinthians 12:9a GNT)

Be careful that none of you fails to respond to the grace which God gives, for if he does there can very easily spring up in him a bitter spirit which is not only bad in itself but can also poison the lives of many others.

(Hebrews 12:15 JBP)

Reflect

One of the most asked questions of the Christian faith is "If God is good, why does He allow suffering?" It's a great question. I've asked it. Have you?

Let me take you back to the very beginning, Genesis 1, when all that God created was perfect. For a time, there was perfect harmony with God and others. Then sin messed that up! As a result, we experience pain here on this broken planet. We are no longer promised an easy life. Sin changed everything. In fact, many around the world suffer daily from the consequences of sin. Disease, betrayal, crime, violence, oppression, addiction, even slavery, are daily battles that many people face. One day God will set things right. In the meantime, we have to figure out how to live like Christ even in our pain.

When and how have you experienced the brokenness of this planet? Give a recent example:

Read 2 Peter 3:9 in the margin. What does this verse teach us about God's plan?

Reread 2 Corinthians 12:9a (page 85). What did the apostle Paul say about grace? How would you define grace in your own words?

Grace is what sustains us in our pain. God's grace, the gift we don't deserve but so desperately need, is our life jacket when we feel that we are drowning in our pain. When we pray in a crisis, God will respond to us in one of two ways. He will either remove the source of pain, or He will give us the strength to go through it. I prefer the first option, don't you? But God does not remove every pain. Sometimes He says gently to us, "I will walk through this with you. I will extend my grace to you in your hurt."

When God's grace meets you in the deep, dark places of your life, nothing—no problem, no crisis, no pain—can devastate your life. You learn that you can handle anything with God's help. In fact, we each can grow and even become a better person on the other side of our pain.

But that isn't always the outcome, is it? Sometimes we handle our problems poorly. Instead of becoming better, bitterness sets in.

Reread Hebrews 12:15 (page 85). What does Paul say can happen if we don't respond to God's grace?

When life is unfair, we have a choice. Will we become bitter or better? The antidote to whatever pain you're facing is God's grace. To respond to or receive the grace of God, all you have to do is humble yourself, tell God you need His help, and receive His grace.

As we've seen this week in our study, our heroine is a little girl who has been snatched from her family in a raid on her village. She is now living as a slave in the home of Naaman. We can conclude that before her kidnapping this child was given a rich legacy of faith because she knows the love and compassion of God. She believes in the power of God to heal. And when the opportunity arises, she shares that love by encouraging her captor to reach out for God's healing touch. In the midst of her pain, she loves. She is a great example of grace in action.

Her situation seems so outrageous—a child slave! But even in our world today this is still happening. There are children kidnapped in Africa where the boys are made into soldiers and the girls are sold as child brides. In Southeast Asia, Central America, and many other areas of the world, including our own country, children are bought and sold in the sex trade. This world is broken! These sins are horrific; and for those caught in these circumstances, life must be horrific. But even in these darkest of situations, God's light can shine.

I have had the privilege to meet a few of the people who have escaped enslaved lives and know the power of Christ's love. They carry emotional and physical wounds from their childhood, but they are not bitter people. In fact, they have chosen to devote their lives to sharing the love of Christ. They want to pass on the very love that sustained them in their terrors—the love that is the only real hope of the world. They have chosen to be better!

We may not have been enslaved, but we've all faced difficult circumstances. When life treats us unfairly, we have a decision to make. Will we allow it to make us bitter, or will we choose to be better? There is an *active* choice to be made here. With God's help we have to choose—

3Praise be to the God and Father of our Lord Jesus Christ, the Father of compassion and the God of all comfort, 4who comforts us in all our troubles, so that we can comfort those in any trouble with the comfort we ourselves receive from God. 5For just as we share abundantly in the sufferings of Christ, so also our comfort abounds through Christ.
(2 Corinthians 1:3-5 NIV)

sometimes repeatedly, sometimes day after day—to release the hurt and forgive those who do not deserve our forgiveness. This is grace.

As God's girls we are commanded to forgive as we have been forgiven. Ephesians 4:32 says, "Be kind to one another, tenderhearted, forgiving one another, as God in Christ forgave you" (ESV). This is an extremely hard task at times. We are not called to overlook or ignore sin, but we are called to offer forgiveness to those who have hurt us, just as our young heroine did toward Naaman.

Is there anyone toward whom you harbor bitterness? If so, what will it take for you to release that bitterness?

Read 2 Corinthians 1:3-5 in the margin. How can you use your hurts to bless others?

When life treats us unjustly, what choice will we make? Will we choose to become better or bitter? God never wants us to waste our hurts. Turning our hearts toward God, and allowing His grace to work in us and then work through us, allows us to use what was meant to harm us as something in which God's love shines through. Friends, let's not be bitter, let's be better!

Pray

- Thank God for His presence in your pain.
- Repent of the hurts you have allowed to turn into bitterness, and ask God to replace those with His healing love.
- Ask God to reveal to you how you could use your hurts to minister to others.

DAY 4

Settle

Take a few brief minutes to express your love for God through music, art, writing, or some other creative outlet. As you create, allow God's presence to penetrate your current situation.

Focus

⁴So Naaman told the king what the young girl from Israel had said. ⁵"Go and visit the prophet," the king of Aram told him. "I will send a letter of introduction for you to take to the king of Israel." So Naaman started out, carrying as gifts 750 pounds of silver, 150 pounds of gold, and ten sets of clothing. ⁶The letter to the king of Israel said: "With this letter I present my servant Naaman. I want you to heal him of his leprosy."

⁷When the king of Israel read the letter, he tore his clothes in dismay and said, "Am I God, that I can give life and take it away? Why is this man asking me to heal someone with leprosy? I can see that he's just trying to pick a fight with me."

⁸But when Elisha, the man of God, heard that the king of Israel had torn his clothes in dismay, he sent this message to him: "Why are you so upset? Send Naaman to me, and he will learn that there is a true prophet here in Israel."

⁹So Naaman went with his horses and chariots and waited at the door of Elisha's house. ¹⁰But Elisha sent a messenger out to him with this message: "Go and wash yourself seven times in the Jordan River. Then your skin will be restored, and you will be healed of your leprosy."

¹¹But Naaman became angry and stalked away. "I thought he would certainly come out to meet me!" he said. "I expected him to wave his hand over the leprosy and call on the name of the LORD his God and heal me! ¹²Aren't the rivers of Damascus, the Abana and the Pharpar, better than any of the rivers of Israel? Why shouldn't I wash in them and be healed?" So Naaman turned and went away in a rage.

¹³But his officers tried to reason with him and said, "Sir, if the prophet had told you to do something very difficult, wouldn't you have done it? So you should certainly obey him when he says simply, 'Go and wash and be

cured!'" *¹⁴So Naaman went down to the Jordan River and dipped himself seven times, as the man of God had instructed him. And his skin became as healthy as the skin of a young child, and he was healed!*

¹⁵Then Naaman and his entire party went back to find the man of God. They stood before him, and Naaman said, "Now I know that there is no God in all the world except in Israel. So please accept a gift from your servant."

(2 Kings 5:4-15)

Reflect

Have you ever had one of those days, that turned into one of those weeks, that turned into one of those prolonged seasons of life? Most of us experience this at least a few times in life. Sometimes it comes about due to an illness or an unpleasable boss or a rebellious child. Maybe your tough season lasted a month, or perhaps it turned into years of turmoil and heartache.

For me, one of those tough seasons occurred early in ministry. A cranky boss, tough workload, long-distance separation from family, and the loss of our first child coincided, and for a while it felt like God had abandoned us. The really tough thing was that Jim was going through a difficult season of life too. It is so much easier to go through hardship when the people closest to you are doing well. That way, one can reach down and lift the other up. Unfortunately, though, this was not our situation. We were both down, and it felt like we would never be up again. We were getting by one day at a time the best we could and wondering, "God, where are you?"

We began to question everything and cry out to God: *Is ministry right for us? Are You trying to redirect us? Have we failed You somehow? This isn't fair!* We asked all the questions and really struggled through this time. The most overwhelming emotion I remember from this time is not anger but just a deep sense of sadness.

A friend came to see us during this time to offer encouragement. I remember he said, "You guys are in a character-building season. My kids just finished a character-building season in soccer. That's the nice way of saying they got beat at every game. But they became better athletes through that process. God is refining you, and He will bring something good out of this if you let Him." Now that may sound great, but it was no comfort at the time. Character-building seasons are tough!

When have you experienced a character-building season?

How did you feel?

How would you hope to handle the next tough season of life?

For our little heroine we've been focusing on this week, it has been more than a character-building season. Her life has been *devastated*. She's been taken from her family and sold into slavery. Perhaps she watched as her parents were killed and her home burned. Most likely she suffers from the savagery she has witnessed.

Put yourself in this slave girl's sandals. What questions must she have asked of God?

Despite her circumstances, God uses her in a powerful way. She will not allow her pain or the pagan culture in which she lives to diminish her faith. It is amazing that she continues to have such a deep belief in the God who did not spare her from slavery. Even more remarkable is that she has the courage to offer a solution to Naaman's leprous condition.

As we read today, the rest of the story is up to Naaman. Will he seek out Elisha, the prophet of the Lord? Will he do what Elisha instructed him to do?

Reread 2 Kings 5:4-14 (pages 89–90). What did the king tell Naaman to do, and what was his response?

What did Elisha tell Naaman to do, and what was his initial response?

How did Naaman's officers convince him to do as Elisha instructed?

We see that the choice to follow through is Naaman's, but let us not forget that the choice to point him to healing in the first place comes from our unnamed little girl!

Reluctantly, Naaman does as Elisha instructs him to do, and his leprosy is miraculously healed. But something even more significant happens.

Reread 2 Kings 5:15 (page 90). What does Naaman come to know?

This powerful military leader who has great favor with the enemy king of Aram comes to know the awesome power of the God of his enemy— the one true God. Through this experience he comes to a faith of his own. Imagine the implications this had for a man of his influence. I like to imagine that Naaman returned and sought out our little servant girl to thank her and talk with her about her amazing God.

Often in Scripture we see heroes of the faith move from ordinary to extraordinary through courage and faith, just as our little handmaiden of Israel does. Like her, centuries later there would be another young maiden, Esther, who would be uniquely placed in a difficult situation. And in her crisis she finds the courage to make a difference.

The Book of Esther tells us the story of a young Jewish woman who becomes the queen of Persia through an interesting beauty pageant of sorts. She rises to a great position in Persia, but her life and the lives of all Jews living there are threatened when the evil prime minster Haman plots to exterminate them. Boldly, Esther goes before her husband, King Xerxes, without being summoned. This was a move that could have resulted in her death because no one was to appear before the king without him calling for him or her. With her cousin Mordecai's encouragement, Esther pleads for the lives of her people at a banquet she hosts for the king.

To see how this story ends, read Esther 7 and 8. It's a dramatic plot twist for the evil Haman—and for Esther's people.

Now put yourself in Esther's place. What fears and concerns would you have had?

How did Esther's bravery impact those around her?

What are the long-lasting implications of Esther's actions?

To all who mourn
in Israel he will give:
beauty for ashes; joy
instead of mourning;
praise instead of
heaviness. For God
has planted them
like strong and
graceful oaks for his
own glory.

(Isaiah 61:3 TLB)

Read Isaiah 61:3 in the margin. How have you seen God bring something beautiful out of hard situations?

In what unique circumstances might God want to use *you* to shine His light?

These two stories teach us several things that we can apply in our lives on a daily basis.

1. *God can use anyone who is willing to be faithful.* Esther and the little maiden lived in different time periods, but their stories show us that as we are faithful to God, He is able to bring blessings from tragedy.

2. *Faithfulness often demands courage.* Esther and our small heroine showed great bravery. Each survived in a foreign land—and Esther even thrived—but they had to show courage in order to be faithful. In 1 Chronicles 28:20 (NIV) we read, "Do not be afraid or discouraged, for the Lord God, my God, is with you." The takeaway for us is to be strong and courageous and do the work, confident that God is always with us.

3. *Our faith can point others to healing grace.* Both of these biblical heroines bravely and faithfully pointed others to the one true God. In Esther's time, healing came as a reprieve from execution; in Aram physical healing was needed. But in each situation there was an even bigger need: spiritual truth and healing.

Whenever we have
the opportunity, we
should do good to
everyone.

(Galatians 6:10)

Read Galatians 6:10 in the margin. What are we to do and when?

The apostle Paul urges us in Galatians to use every opportunity we have, even the painful ones that come in our character-building seasons, to do good to others. Through these practical demonstrations of love, we bless others and honor God.

Through our faith and courage, God is able to use us in very difficult situations. As I look back on the character-building season I mentioned earlier, I see that God was toughening us up. Although He did not cause the pain Jim and I were enduring, He also did not waste it. He taught us that in the hard times you press on; that life and ministry are not always easy; and that in the low times faithfulness and fierce tenacity are required. I would not want to repeat that particular character-building season, but I am thankful for the lessons it taught us.

Seek Him daily and ask Him to bring beauty from the ashes of your life too. And remember, despite the hard times we go through, God is able to heal, deliver, and bring blessing.

Pray

- As you reflect on the tough seasons of your life, ask God to completely heal any lingering hurts that remain.
- Listen to "Beauty from Ashes" recorded by Chris McClarney (or another relevant song of your choice).
- Thank God for His faithfulness during your hard times.
- Seek His will in how He would use you to reach out to others today.

DAY 5

Settle

Anxiety can rob us of peace. As you take time to slow your thoughts today, ask God to drive out all worry and fear and give you peace so that you may focus on Him alone in these next moments.

Focus

¹⁴*Then Jesus returned to Galilee, filled with the Holy Spirit's power. Reports about him spread quickly through the whole region.* ¹⁵*He taught regularly in their synagogues and was praised by everyone.*

¹⁶*When he came to the village of Nazareth, his boyhood home, he went as usual to the synagogue on the Sabbath and stood up to read the Scriptures.* ¹⁷*The scroll of Isaiah the prophet was handed to him. He unrolled the scroll and found the place where this was written:*

¹⁸*"The Spirit of the L*ORD *is upon me,*
> *for he has anointed me to bring Good News to the poor.*
He has sent me to proclaim that captives will be released,
> *that the blind will see,*
> *that the oppressed will be set free,*
¹⁹*and that the time of the L*ORD*'s favor has come."*

²⁰*He rolled up the scroll, handed it back to the attendant, and sat down. All eyes in the synagogue looked at him intently.* ²¹*Then he began to speak to them. "The Scripture you've just heard has been fulfilled this very day!"*

²²*Everyone spoke well of him and was amazed by the gracious words that came from his lips. "How can this be?" they asked. "Isn't this Joseph's son?"*

²³*Then he said, "You will undoubtedly quote me this proverb: 'Physician, heal yourself'—meaning, 'Do miracles here in your hometown like those you did in Capernaum.'* ²⁴*But I tell you the truth, no prophet is accepted in his own hometown.*

²⁵*"Certainly there were many needy widows in Israel in Elijah's time, when the heavens were closed for three and a half years, and a severe famine*

devastated the land. [26]Yet Elijah was not sent to any of them. He was sent instead to a foreigner—a widow of Zarephath in the land of Sidon. [27]And many in Israel had leprosy in the time of the prophet Elisha, but the only one healed was Naaman, a Syrian."

[28]When they heard this, the people in the synagogue were furious. [29]Jumping up, they mobbed him and forced him to the edge of the hill on which the town was built. They intended to push him over the cliff, [30]but he passed right through the crowd and went on his way.

(Luke 4:14-30)

Reflect

When I was a little girl, my parents often taught me to "err on the side of generosity." It's a mantra that has stayed with me throughout my life. Whether it's helping someone on the side of the road needing assistance, leaving a tip for a server in a restaurant, or selecting a gift for a friend, erring on the side of generosity is a good habit to develop.

But what about erring on the side of generosity when it comes to things that cost a lot more than money—things such as sharing our time, our forgiveness, or our faith. Personally, I've found that it is easier to leave a big tip than to offer these types of generosity.

Doing the right thing in difficult circumstances is hard. But it's one of the things that sets those with a fierce faith apart from the pack. Forgiving when the wound is deep, sharing our faith when it feels awkward, and slowing down to make time for others are all ways of being generous with those around us. John Wesley, founder of the Methodist movement, is often credited with saying:

> *Do all the good you can,*
> *By all the means you can,*
> *In all the ways you can,*
> *In all the places you can,*
> *At all the times you can,*
> *To all the people you can,*
> *As long as ever you can.*

I like that. It's poetic. It's noble. But it is not convenient. It is not easy. Fierce women of God do the hard things. They *err on the side of generosity* because they know that they are living for more than the trivial. They are fighting a battle that is worthy. They suit up with the shield of faith and the helmet of salvation and do the hard things!

Fierce women of God know that their identities are wrapped up in their relationship with Christ and not the approval of others, and that is freeing. It frees us to give others what they simply do not deserve. In return, we need no credit or accolades because the act of generosity is enough.

Our unnamed heroine, Naaman's slave girl, does the hard thing. As we have learned this week, she is held captive by foreigners who have ripped her from her home. But in a difficult circumstance she offers hope, healing, and love. She shares not only practical information that leads to Naaman's healing but also the very hope of salvation. By sending Naaman to meet Elisha, she exposes her master to the love and power of God.

So, let's make this personal. What holds you captive? Maybe it's anger toward someone in your past. Perhaps it's an addiction or emotional stronghold such as depression or loneliness. Perhaps it is just fear—fear of what might happen if you step out in faith.

What holds you captive?

How might it be impacting your testimony?

How might others benefit if you began to err on the side of generosity?

What would you need to do differently to make this happen?

We've seen this week that this little girl errs on the side of generosity in an unwelcome and painful situation. That is amazing. Equally amazing is that God heals this pagan commander of an enemy army. This little girl points Naaman to the prophet Elisha; and Elisha, through the power of God, heals him! Incredible. This is a man who has led raids against Elisha's own people—God's chosen people! Yet God loves Naaman and shows him mercy.

This foreign soldier, Naaman, is mentioned again in the Bible in an interesting place. We read of him as Jesus begins his ministry in his hometown of Nazareth. Jesus is just beginning his ministry; and yet his very own people, those who have watched him grow up, do not receive Him. He is rejected in his own hometown.

Reread Luke 4:14-30 (pages 96–97). What does this passage teach us about faith and miracles?

This could have been a tremendous moment for the people of Nazareth, but instead of embracing Jesus as the Messiah, they threaten to kill Him. There is no faith there, and as a result there are no miracles recorded. It is in this moment that Jesus points to other times in Israel's history when God's people did not believe; and because of their unbelief, miracles were rare in Israel and the prophets were sent by God to other places instead.

Look again at verses 25-26. When there was a famine in the land, where was Elijah sent to minister—and to whom?

During the prophet Elijah's time, when the people of God were worshiping Baal and pagan idols, the people of God suffered. Yet Elijah was sent to Sidon, located in modern-day Lebanon, to care for the needs of a widow there.

We see something similar with the prophet Elisha, who was the attendant and disciple of Elijah before his death.

Now look at verse 27. Whom did Elisha heal when many in Israel had leprosy?

Elisha lived in Israel where there were many suffering with leprosy, yet apparently he was not instructed by God to deliver them from this dreaded disease. Instead, he responded to the request of an enemy commander of war—a man who had traveled from the area that is modern-day Syria to seek his help. What a paradox it is for Elijah, Elisha, and our heroine maiden to extend love and healing in foreign places. This is, perhaps, erring on the side of generosity at its best.

Why do you think these three extended this kind of love and grace to foreigners?

How and to whom is God calling *you* to err on the side of generosity?

Fierce conjures up images of strength, but strength comes in many forms. Our heroine this week is just a child; but as we've highlighted again and again, she is a child with a fierce faith. She is generous, compassionate, and brave enough to speak up when needed. Let's seek to live into this type of fierce faith—one that steps into tough situations and points people to God's healing power.

Pray

- If possible, listen to Jesus Culture's recording of the song "Fierce." God's love for you, my friend, is fierce! Allow these words to speak to your heart today.
- Thank God for His grace in your life.
- Seek how God would use you today to err on the side of generosity.

Video Viewer Guide: Week 3

Now Naaman was commander of the army of the king of Aram. He was a great man in the sight of his master and highly regarded, because through him the LORD had given victory to Aram. He was a valiant soldier, but he had leprosy.

Now bands of raiders from Aram had gone out and had taken captive a young girl from Israel, and she served Naaman's wife. She said to her mistress, "If only my master would see the prophet who is in Samaria! He would cure him of his leprosy."

Naaman went to his master and told him what the girl from Israel had said. "By all means, go," the king of Aram replied. "I will send a letter to the king of Israel." So Naaman left, taking with him ten talents of silver, six thousand shekels of gold and ten sets of clothing. The letter that he took to the king of Israel read: "With this letter I am sending my servant Naaman to you so that you may cure him of his leprosy."

As soon as the king of Israel read the letter, he tore his robes and said, "Am I God? Can I kill and bring back to life? Why does this fellow send someone to me to be cured of his leprosy?" (2 Kings 5:1-7 NIV)

"I thought that he would surely come out to me and stand and call on the name of the LORD his God, wave his hand over the spot and cure me of my leprosy. Are not Abana and Pharpar, the rivers of Damascus, better than all the waters of Israel? Couldn't I wash in them and be cleansed?" So he turned and went off in a rage. (2 Kings 5:11-12 NIV)

"Love your enemies! Pray for those who persecute you! In that way, you will be acting as true children of your Father in heaven." (Matthew 5:44-45)

"To you who are ready for the truth, I say this: Love your enemies. Let them bring out the best in you, not the worst. When someone gives you a hard time, respond with the energies of prayer for that person. If someone slaps you in the face, stand there and take it. If someone grabs your shirt, giftwrap your best coat and make a present of it. If someone takes unfair advantage of you, use the occasion to practice the servant life. . . .

"I tell you, love your enemies. Help and give without expecting a return. You'll never—I promise—regret it. Live out this God-created identity the way our Father lives toward us, generously and graciously, even when we're at our worst. Our Father is kind; you be kind.

"Don't pick on people, jump on their failures, criticize their faults—unless, of course, you want the same treatment. Don't condemn those who are down; that hardness can boomerang.

Video Viewer Guide: Week 3

Be easy on people; you'll find life a lot easier. Give away your life; you'll find life given back, but not merely given back—given back with bonus and blessing. Giving, not getting, is the way. Generosity begets generosity." (Luke 6: 27-30, 35-38 MSG)

We are to show _____ to those who are _____ to us.

Two things I am convinced that we cannot fully comprehend this side of heaven are how horrible the _____ in our lives looks to God and how deeply He _____ us.

Week 4

The Samaritan Woman

John 4

DAY 1

Settle

As you quiet yourself to spend some quality time with Jesus, recall a time when you were very thirsty. Do you remember the sensation when you finally had something cool to drink? Satisfying, thirst-quenching, refreshing. Allow this time today to refresh you in that same type of way—to renew you and quench your soul with God's sweetness.

Focus

[1]Jesus knew the Pharisees had heard that he was baptizing and making more disciples than John [2](though Jesus himself didn't baptize them—his disciples did). [3]So he left Judea and returned to Galilee.

[4]He had to go through Samaria on the way. [5]Eventually he came to the Samaritan village of Sychar, near the field that Jacob gave to his son Joseph. [6]Jacob's well was there; and Jesus, tired from the long walk, sat wearily beside the well about noontime. [7]Soon a Samaritan woman came to draw water, and Jesus said to her, "Please give me a drink." [8]He was alone at the time because his disciples had gone into the village to buy some food.

[9]The woman was surprised, for Jews refuse to have anything to do with Samaritans. She said to Jesus, "You are a Jew, and I am a Samaritan woman. Why are you asking me for a drink?"

[10]Jesus replied, "If you only knew the gift God has for you and who you are speaking to, you would ask me, and I would give you living water."

[11]"But sir, you don't have a rope or a bucket," she said, "and this well is very deep. Where would you get this living water? [12]And besides, do you think you're greater than our ancestor Jacob, who gave us this well? How can you offer better water than he and his sons and his animals enjoyed?"

[13]Jesus replied, "Anyone who drinks this water will soon become thirsty again. [14]But those who drink the water I give will never be thirsty again. It becomes a fresh, bubbling spring within them, giving them eternal life."

[15]"Please, sir," the woman said, "give me this water! Then I'll never be thirsty again, and I won't have to come here to get water."

[16]"Go and get your husband," Jesus told her.

[17]"I don't have a husband," the woman replied.

Jesus said, "You're right! You don't have a husband—[18]for you have had five husbands, and you aren't even married to the man you're living with now. You certainly spoke the truth!"

[19]"Sir," the woman said, "you must be a prophet. [20]So tell me, why is it that you Jews insist that Jerusalem is the only place of worship, while we Samaritans claim it is here at Mount Gerizim, where our ancestors worshiped?"

[21]Jesus replied, "Believe me, dear woman, the time is coming when it will no longer matter whether you worship the Father on this mountain or in Jerusalem. [22]You Samaritans know very little about the one you worship, while we Jews know all about him, for salvation comes through the Jews. [23]But the time is coming—indeed it's here now—when true worshipers will worship the Father in spirit and in truth. The Father is looking for those who will worship him that way. [24]For God is Spirit, so those who worship him must worship in spirit and in truth."

[25]The woman said, "I know the Messiah is coming—the one who is called Christ. When he comes, he will explain everything to us."

[26]Then Jesus told her, "I AM the Messiah!"

(John 4:1-26)

Reflect

So far in our study we have been examining the stories of some of the lesser-known women in the Old Testament—Shiphrah and Puah, Deborah, and Naaman's servant girl. This week we turn to the New Testament. Many of us have examined the stories of women such as Elizabeth, Martha, and the three Marys—Jesus' mother, the sister of Martha, and Mary Magdalene. But there are stories in the New Testament of lesser-known women who also have something to teach us about what it means to be a fierce woman of God. In the remaining weeks of our study we will consider four of these women: the woman of Samaria who met Jesus at a well; Dorcas, who cared for those in need; and Lois and Eunice, a mother-daughter team who are commended for raising young Timothy in faith. Are you ready to get started?

This week we're considering the Samaritan woman. Though you may be familiar with the story found in John 4, she's "lesser known" because we don't know much about her. But before we dive in to her story, I want to share a personal story with you.

One day I had a sore throat, so I went to see my physician. She's a delightful person who has become a friend over the years. Usually, I have to wait a while to see her, but on this day she had me ushered right in, coming into the exam room almost immediately. When she entered I expected to get down to the business of my illness, but instead she pulled up a chair and said, "I am so glad you're here today. I think you are the one who is supposed to interpret my dream!"

Now, I love Jesus, but interpreting dreams is not on my résumé. I mean, I'm not Joseph; what do I know about dreams?

My doctor is from another country and is not a follower of Christ. Having shared my faith with her before, I knew that her belief system was grounded in science—what she could study and explain. As I was quickly going through my options of how to respond to her, I thought, "Well, she seems pretty convinced I'm supposed to listen to her. Why not?" So I said, "Well, I don't know if I can interpret your dream or not, but why don't you share it and we'll see what happens."

So she began, "In my dream I was in a desert, and there were people all around me dying. They were so thirsty. I was trying to save them all. There was a small mud puddle in the sand, so I would scoop up as much liquid as I could and give it to them. But it was never enough. They continued to die, and I was exhausted. But then your man walked up."

"My man?" I asked. "You mean my husband?"

"No, not him. You know, your man."

I did know who she meant now, but I wanted to hear her say it. So I responded, "Who?"

"You know who!" she said.

"Say his name," I prodded gently. And reluctantly she did: "Jesus, it was Jesus! He walked up to me and said, 'This water is drying up. What they need is living water. Give them living water.'"

And then, she said, she woke up. She continued, "Do you know what the Living Water is? Is that a thing for you people?" she asked.

Now, as I said before, I'm no Joseph, but this dream seemed pretty clear to me.

"Yes, actually I do know about Living Water," I told her. "Let me show you."

I pulled out my phone and through the Bible app shared with her the story we're studying this week.

She was teary as I shared, so I'm thinking, OK, *this is going to be a great moment*. I'm going to get to lead her to Christ right here. Maybe God is going to use my sore throat and her dream to do something incredible! So I asked her, "What do you want to do with this sweet gift of a dream God has given you? How do you think He wants you to respond?"

She cast her eyes down and said, "I don't know. My faith is in my science. I just don't know." And at least for now, that's where the story ends. Yet her story isn't over!

John's story about a Samaritan woman who encounters Jesus, on the other hand, has a different ending.

In the heat of the day, Jesus meets a woman of Samaria at a well and does something shocking. He speaks to her. As we will see, a Jewish man speaking to a Samaritan—especially a woman—is just not done. But Jesus breaks that barrier and asks her for a drink of water. It is a simple request that begins an honest dialogue and ultimately leads her to faith in Jesus.

As we explore her story more deeply this week, we will concentrate on how

- Jesus has come to reach people who are trapped in their sins;
- He offers us more than earthly comforts;
- we can move past critics and insecurities to share God's love; and
- we have the responsibility to go and share once we have met Jesus for ourselves.

For today, though, let's just linger in the story and get a feel for the depth of love this passage shows us.

Reread John 4:1-4 (page 105). Where was Jesus going, and where did he have to pass through according to verse 4?

The text says, "He had to go through Samaria." Geographically speaking, this isn't true. There are other routes to be taken from Judea in the south to Galilee in the north. But Jesus ventures west to go through Samaria. He doesn't head up the flat ground of Jordan in the river valley but traverses the mountains to go through Samaria on his way to the sea. There must have been other reasons for Him to travel this route.

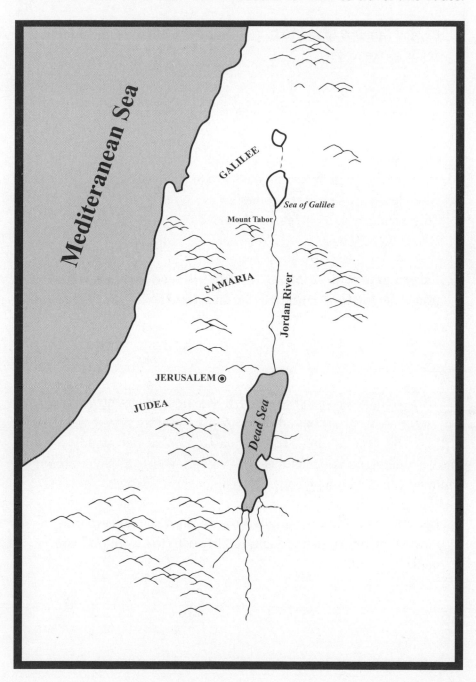

I like to think it was so that He could have this encounter with this woman of Samaria.

Going through Samaria was not a popular route for Jews to take because of its inhabitants.

Reread John 4:9 (page 105). Why was the woman surprised that Jesus spoke to her?

The Samaritan people and the Jews did not associate with each other, as this verse plainly states. What a surprise it must have been for her when Jesus spoke directly to her.

This woman who meets Jesus at the well is not only a Samaritan; she also has a sketchy past.

Reread John 4:16-17 (pages 105–106). What does Jesus reveal about her past and current living situation?

Just then his disciples came back. They were shocked to find him talking to a woman, but none of them had the nerve to ask, "What do you want with her?" or "Why are you talking to her?"

(John 4:27)

This woman has been married five times and is now living with another man. It would be rare for a man to address a woman in public in this time and culture, especially a woman of her standing. So in this encounter where Jesus meets a woman who is a Samaritan and a shunned sinner, you might say He has met the social taboo trifecta.

Read John 4:27 in the margin. How do the disciples respond when they return to find Jesus talking with the woman at the well?

The disciples are shocked to find Jesus engaged in conversation with a Samaritan woman, but Jesus is not concerned with what others are thinking. His concentration is on restoring her into a right relationship with God. Jesus shows love for her—real love that speaks the hard truths and then comes alongside to bring restoration and wholeness. Perhaps Jesus "had to go through Samaria" because this encounter was so important, so desperately needed, for this woman—and for you and me.

Read John 3:16-17 in the margin. Whom does God so love, and what did God's love prompt Him to do?

16For God so loved the world that he gave his one and only Son, that whoever believes in him shall not perish but have eternal life. 17For God did not send his Son into the world to condemn the world, but to save the world through him.
(John 3:16-17 NIV)

You are included in those God so loved. Write your name in the verse below to make it more personal for you:

For God so loved _____ that He gave his one and only Son. . . .

How have you felt God go out of His way to show you love in the past?

For whom might you go out of your way to show love today?

I'm not sure if it is because of my doctor's dream, because this story is about a female sinner, or both, but I feel a real personal connection to Jesus' encounter with the woman of Samaria. As we delve into this passage this week, put yourself in the story. Make it your personal encounter too. Jesus waited by that well for her two thousand years ago, and He waits for you today.

Pray

- Listen to "You Say" recorded by Lauren Daigle (or another relevant song of your choice) as you enter into prayer.
- Thank God for who He says you are, in contrast to who the world may say you are.
- Ask Him for wisdom in how you might love on others today.
- Pray for those needing peace, forgiveness, and hope in our world.

DAY 2

Settle

Meditate on Matthew 19:26 for a few moments: "Jesus looked at them intently and said, 'Humanly speaking, it is impossible. But with God everything is possible.'" Whatever may be troubling you today, give it to God. Take Him at His word: *all things are possible through God.*

Focus

⁴He had to go through Samaria on the way. ⁵Eventually he came to the Samaritan village of Sychar, near the field that Jacob gave to his son Joseph. ⁶Jacob's well was there; and Jesus, tired from the long walk, sat wearily beside the well about noontime. ⁷Soon a Samaritan woman came to draw water, and Jesus said to her, "Please give me a drink." ⁸He was alone at the time because his disciples had gone into the village to buy some food.

⁹The woman was surprised, for Jews refuse to have anything to do with Samaritans. She said to Jesus, "You are a Jew, and I am a Samaritan woman. Why are you asking me for a drink?"

¹⁰Jesus replied, "If you only knew the gift God has for you and who you are speaking to, you would ask me, and I would give you living water."

¹¹"But sir, you don't have a rope or a bucket," she said, "and this well is very deep. Where would you get this living water? ¹²And besides, do you think you're greater than our ancestor Jacob, who gave us this well? How can you offer better water than he and his sons and his animals enjoyed?"

¹³Jesus replied, "Anyone who drinks this water will soon become thirsty again. ¹⁴But those who drink the water I give will never be thirsty again. It becomes a fresh, bubbling spring within them, giving them eternal life."

¹⁵"Please, sir," the woman said, "give me this water! Then I'll never be thirsty again, and I won't have to come here to get water."

¹⁶"Go and get your husband," Jesus told her.

¹⁷"I don't have a husband," the woman replied.

Jesus said, "You're right! You don't have a husband—¹⁸for you have had five husbands, and you aren't even married to the man you're living with now. You certainly spoke the truth!"

(John 4:4-18)

In your hearts revere Christ as Lord. Always be prepared to give an answer to everyone who asks you to give the reason for the hope that you have. But do this with gentleness and respect.

(1 Peter 3:15 NIV)

Reflect

It was meant to be critical, but it's one of the greatest compliments our church has ever received. "They just let anybody in there." Yup! That's exactly right; no matter what your baggage, habits, or hang-ups may be, you are welcome at our church. My husband often tells the crowd, "You're welcome here just as you are, but we're going to love you deeply enough to speak truth into your life." This is Jesus' message: love people deeply.

That's what happens in this beautiful encounter in John 4.

Jesus speaks directly to this woman of Samaria. In the time and culture where this encounter took place, it was unheard of for a Jewish man to speak to a woman in a public setting, especially a Samaritan woman. But Jesus greets her with kindness. He is honest with her, yet his rebuke is not condemning—just convicting. He leaves her with hope, not shame. He treats her with respect.

Sometimes we get respect confused with acceptance. Respect does not necessitate agreeing with everything a person says or does. It certainly doesn't mean we put a stamp of approval on sinful behavior. It does, however, involve treating every person with dignity and love. Jesus is polite in this encounter. He deals with her directly, honestly, and kindly; and as a result, this interaction is effective in changing her life— and ultimately the lives of many others.

Direct, honest, and kind—I love that! Recently, a friend in ministry pointed out to me that we Christians often only do two of these three things when interacting with others. We may be kind and direct, but we don't deal with the honest truths. Or we may be kind and honest, but we don't go directly to the person with whom we should be speaking (and that's gossip, by the way). Or we may be direct and honest, leaving kindness by the wayside. This last combo can often be mean-spirited. But when we strike the balance of direct, honest, and kind, we can avoid the wake of collateral damage that follows unkind exchanges.

Direct, honest, and kind—which of these three do you leave out most often in your interactions with others?

How could it improve your life (and the lives of those around you) if you incorporated a balance of the three?

Taking the initiative and becoming intentional about how, when, and where we interact with people can help us become more loving and effective in our interactions. This is so important because even when we have great intentions, we can do more harm than good if we don't plan carefully how we interact with others.

Jesus wants to redeem this woman whose life has become such a mess, so He is strategic in the details.

Where.

> Now he had to go through Samaria. So he came to a town in Samaria called Sychar, near the plot of ground Jacob had given to his son Joseph. Jacob's well was there, and Jesus, tired as he was from the journey, sat down by the well.
>
> (John 4:4-5 NIV)

I love that Jesus meets this woman at the well—a place that is part of her daily routine as she draws water for everyday necessities. I like to think that He leans up against the well and is waiting for her specifically.

When.

> It was about noon.
>
> (John 4:6 NIV)

The Scripture is specific in telling us it is noon, the heat of the day. Gathering water at this time of day would not have been the custom.

Women—typically the younger women—would go to the well either early or late in the day to avoid the heat and to socialize. Her arrival at noon indicates that she most likely is trying to avoid the social gathering. Perhaps as a woman who has been married five times previously and now is living with someone else, she has been shunned or even ridiculed in Samaria. Making her journey to the well at noon, she avoids the crowds and the whispers. It also allows Jesus to speak to her privately.

How.

When a Samaritan woman came to draw water, Jesus said to her, "Will you give me a drink?"

(John 4:7 NIV)

We have already said that Jesus is direct, honest, and kind. But let's take note of a few other dynamics.

Jesus takes the initiative. He engages first. A common phrase around our home is "Be friendly first." It actually is a valuable life tool when used wisely as we share love with others.

Jesus piques her interest. He doesn't jump straight to accusations and never becomes condemning. Instead, He offers her something of interest—a lifetime supply of the very thing she is there to collect.

Jesus shows that He knows her life and is interested in her situation.

Sharing the love of God is not just a responsibility we have as followers of Christ; it is a privilege. We are called to reach out to messy people, inviting them into our homes and churches and offering them genuine love. So, taking the time to think through the specifics of how we interact and how we handle conversations—especially difficult and important ones—is critical. Being intentional about the where, when, and how will make you more effective and convincing as you live into your call as a Christ follower.

One of my favorite definitions of evangelism is "one beggar telling another beggar where to find bread."[1] We also could replace "bread" with "water." This definition is not high and mighty. It reminds us of who we are and what we have received. We are not the bread-makers; we don't own the bakery. Nor are we the water source. We are simply people in need who have something that others also need. And we're called to share it!

Reread Romans 3:23 and 1 John 1:8 in the margin. With these verses in mind, what should our attitude be toward our own sin and the sins of others?

For all have sinned and fall short of the glory of God.
(Romans 3:23 NIV)

If we say we have no sin, we deceive ourselves, and the truth is not in us.
(1 John 1:8 ESV)

How could you be more available to those trapped in sin who may be living far from God?

Where might you position yourself in the way that Jesus positioned Himself at the well?

Reread 1 Peter 3:15 (page 114). What does this verse encourage us to do, and why?

Take the time now to write a short version of your testimony—one that, when the opportunity presents itself, you could share in about five to eight minutes, with gentleness and respect.

Throughout the Gospels we see Jesus is criticized for interacting with people of less than stellar reputations. Read

[10]Later, Matthew invited Jesus and his disciples to his home as dinner guests, along with many tax collectors and other disreputable sinners. [11]But when the Pharisees saw this, they asked his disciples, "Why does your teacher eat with such scum?"

[12]When Jesus heard this, he said, "Healthy people don't need a doctor—sick people do."

(Matthew 9:10-12)

Matthew 9:10-12 in the margin. How does Jesus respond, and what does this reveal about His heart and mission?

"They just let anybody in there." It's not such a bad commentary on the attitude that the church and we as Christians are supposed to have. Meeting people right where they are and then loving them enough to speak the truth into their lives is what we are called to do as followers of Christ. Again, loving others is not condoning sin. Far from it. It means being committed to developing the skills necessary to be honest, direct, and kind—and strategically investing our lives in loving others and helping them to find the Bread of Life and Living Water, Jesus.

Pray

- Thank God for the sweet and undeserved gift of grace and salvation.
- Meditate on how and to whom He is calling you to show love.
- Lift up your failures to God, asking for and receiving forgiveness and knowing that He loves you.

DAY 3

Settle

As you begin to settle in for some intentional time with God today, grab a cold cup of water. Hold it, sip it, and allow it to refresh you. As you drink, imagine that the coolness of that water is God's very Spirit flowing in and through you as you focus on Him.

Focus

[10]Jesus answered her, "If you knew the gift of God and who it is that asks you for a drink, you would have asked him and he would have given you living water."

[11]"Sir," the woman said, "you have nothing to draw with and the well is deep. Where can you get this living water? [12]Are you greater than our father Jacob, who gave us the well and drank from it himself, as did also his sons and his livestock?"

[13]Jesus answered, "Everyone who drinks this water will be thirsty again, [14]but whoever drinks the water I give them will never thirst. Indeed, the water I give them will become in them a spring of water welling up to eternal life."

[15]The woman said to him, "Sir, give me this water so that I won't get thirsty and have to keep coming here to draw water."

(John 4:10-15 NIV)

[37]On the last day, the climax of the festival, Jesus stood and shouted to the crowds, "Anyone who is thirsty may come to me! [38]Anyone who believes in me may come and drink! For the Scriptures declare, 'Rivers of living water will flow from his heart.'"

(John 7:37-38)

Reflect

The water from Jacob's Well is the sweetest I've ever tasted. It is clean and pure and very cold. I know this because a few years ago while traveling through Israel, I was insistent that we take a trip into Samaria to visit Jacob's Well. Our guide discouraged us at first because Samaria is in the West Bank, a Palestinian-occupied section of Israel that is the home of thousands of refugees and is sometimes a volatile place. But just as some people on our trip were set on visiting Nazareth, Bethlehem, or the garden tomb, I was determined to drink from the well where Jesus encountered the woman from Samaria.

There are a few spots in the Holy Land that we know for certain are exact locations where Jesus was at one time. In Bethlehem there is a spot attributed to his birth, but we cannot be sure that it is the exact location. In Jerusalem there are several gardens that may be the location of the tomb, but there is no certainty of this. But in a few cases, we know for sure: this is it. This is where Jesus actually walked or taught. Jacob's Well is one of those places, and it is truly a special place.

The well, which is thousands of years old, is now far below ground level. You actually go into a church that has been built on top of the well and descend stairs to a cellar-type room in order to get to this rock-hewn, ancient water source.

As I stood in that room, I thought of the power of this water. Life in ancient Israel revolved around water sources. It was essential to daily life—for bathing, watering crops and livestock, cooking, and of course drinking. Water was life-giving. And since the Middle East has so few clean water sources, a well like this one in Samaria would have been a very popular spot. Surely its primary function was to supply water; but as we see in Scripture, it also would have served as a social setting.

In the 1950s young men and women hung out at soda shops and sock hops. Today young people meet up at sporting events and movie theaters. But in ancient Israel wells seemed to have been the happening place. Rebekah meets Abraham's servant who is looking for a wife for Isaac at a well in Genesis 24:10-27; Moses meets his wife, Zipporah, at a well in Exodus 2:15-22; and Saul meets some young woman at the well while looking for his father's donkeys in 1 Samuel 9:3-12. Wells were a popular place to socialize.

As mentioned yesterday, the usual time for gathering the water would have been early in the morning or near sunset, but the meeting we're studying this week occurred during the heat of the day—a time when the well area most likely would have been deserted.

As I imagine the scene, I see Jesus propped up against the well in the noonday heat just waiting to have this life-altering conversation with a woman who needs real love in her life. (In fact, when I imagine this scene, I like to picture Him waiting there for *me*. I encourage you to do the same.) The disciples have gone to find lunch. So, here they are, Jesus and the woman of Samaria. As far as we know, it's just the two of them there as they have this honest, raw, and life-changing conversation.

Imagine yourself walking up to the well and finding Jesus waiting for you. How would you feel meeting Him face-to-face? Would you have any fears, and if so, what would they be?

What would you hope to talk about? What would you want to ask Him?

Reread John 4:10-14 (page 119). What does Jesus say about living water in comparison to the water in the well?

Think carefully for a moment. What are you really thirsty for in life? (Consider what consumes your thought life and your time as you answer this question.)

Is your "thirst" or longing for friends, significance, control, happiness, a better tennis stroke, good looks, an improved marriage, a healthy relationship with your kids, a raise, or to lose weight?

We all thirst for things in life. But so many of the things we thirst for never fully satisfy us. As the desire for these things overtakes our desire for God, we fall into a trap; and it leaves us with a thirst that can never be quenched. Thirsting for things over our desire for God actually has a nasty little name: sin. And sin is addictive. We thirst for something; we crave it. But even when we have it, we aren't satisfied. Like the alcoholic who needs one more drink, the smoker who craves the next cigarette, the social media diva who needs to check the number of likes, or the businessperson who is addicted to the thrill of the deal, we stay thirsty for more and are never really satisfied. Jesus warns of this: "Everyone who drinks this water will be thirsty again." But when our desire is for Christ, our thirst is quenched. The well that springs up within us when we accept Jesus' gift of living water brings eternal peace.

The imagery of living water is used numerous times throughout Scripture. In John 7 we read:

> On the last and greatest day of the festival, Jesus stood and shouted to the crowds, "Anyone who is thirsty may come to me! Anyone who believes in me may come and drink! For the Scriptures declare, 'Rivers of living water will flow from his heart.'" (v. 38)

And in Jeremiah 17:13 we read:

> O Lord, the hope of Israel,
>   all who turn away from you will be disgraced.
> They will be buried in the dust of the earth,
>   for they have abandoned the Lord, the fountain of living water.

Read these other passages that refer to living water, and record your thoughts about each below:

Zechariah 14:8-9

Revelation 7:13-17

Revelation 21:6-8

How might this living water that the Scriptures describe meet your "thirst" mentioned above?

How might it meet your deepest longing?

Once a young woman came to me very sincerely and said, "I just don't know what to do. I simply don't have much of a desire to know God. But I want to." I so appreciated the honest and broken heart from which this was spoken. We prayed and asked God to give her a desire to know Him, a rich desire to be in Scripture, and a desire to live a life that pleased Him. This became her earnest prayer. She began to seek what she didn't yet have, and through the seeking she began to find what she was looking for. Together we believed that God would honor His word in Matthew 7:7.

Read Matthew 7:7 in the margin. What promises does Jesus make in this verse?

"Keep on asking, and you will receive what you ask for. Keep on seeking, and you will find. Keep on knocking, and the door will be opened to you."

(Matthew 7:7)

These are such rich promises from God: ask and you will receive, seek and you will find, knock and the door will be opened.

We often ask, seek, and knock in the all the wrong places. We try to fill our emptiness, to quench our thirst; but without Christ, the emptiness will always return.

Blessed are those
who hunger
and thirst for
righteousness,
    for they will be
filled.
   (Matthew 5:6 NIV)

Jesus knew when He encountered the woman at the well that she needed living water. So, he offered her a drink—pure and clean, living and active—that would satisfy fully, forever.

Read Matthew 5:6 in the margin. According to this verse, what is the blessing we receive when we thirst for the righteousness of Jesus, our Living Water?

As we will see tomorrow, once she receives this living water, she is *changed*. And from that change she is excited to share what she has found with others.

Jesus offers you that same living water today. Drink deeply!

Pray

- Pray back to God this Scripture today, personalizing it even more if you like:

Lord, You said, "Anyone who is thirsty may come to me! Anyone who believes in me may come and drink! For the Scriptures declare, 'Rivers of living water will flow from his heart'" (John 7:37-38). So today I ask You to give me a deep desire to thirst after You and Your will in my life. Fill me with your living water, rich and pure, so that it will flow freely from my heart. Amen.

DAY 4

Settle

Take out a journal and list some of the people who have influenced your spiritual journey in positive ways. Thank God for placing them in your life and for their courage to reach out to you in faith. Begin your time today in praise for who God is and those He has placed in your path to encourage you over the years.

Focus

39"Come and see," he said. It was about four o'clock in the afternoon when they went with him to the place where he was staying, and they remained with him the rest of the day.

40Andrew, Simon Peter's brother, was one of these men who heard what John said and then followed Jesus. 41Andrew went to find his brother, Simon, and told him, "We have found the Messiah" (which means "Christ"). . . .

45Philip went to look for Nathanael and told him, "We have found the very person Moses and the prophets wrote about! His name is Jesus, the son of Joseph from Nazareth."

46"Nazareth!" exclaimed Nathanael. "Can anything good come from Nazareth?"

"Come and see for yourself," Philip replied.

(John 1:39-41, 45-46)

25The woman said, "I know that Messiah" (called Christ) "is coming. When he comes, he will explain everything to us."

26Then Jesus declared, "I, the one speaking to you—I am he."

27Just then his disciples returned and were surprised to find him talking with a woman. But no one asked, "What do you want?" or "Why are you talking with her?"

28Then, leaving her water jar, the woman went back to the town and said to the people, 29"Come, see a man who told me everything I ever did. Could this be the Messiah?" 30They came out of the town and made their way toward him.

(John 4:25-30 NIV)

Reflect

I've been speaking and sharing Christ in groups since I was a teenager. Sometimes the group has been just a few people, but often the crowds have been much larger. I actually love sharing about Jesus and bringing God's Word to life for people. So, it's odd that one of my greatest struggles—a fear, really—is being in front of people. In fact, I sometimes think this panicky feeling is God's way of keeping me humble, on my toes, and reliant on Him. Even today, right before I get up to speak I have a sinking feeling of doubt and panic.

Early in my life when the opportunity to speak came and my panic began, God and I had a conversation that went something like this.

Me: "I can't do this!"
God: "Yes, you can."
Me: "No, I don't want them looking at me, and I don't really have anything worthwhile to say anyway."
God: "So, this is about you? I thought it was about Me."
Me: "Oh, yeah. Sorry about that."

From that experience, and several like it (because sometimes I'm a slow learner), I developed a few phrases that help me when my nerves try to take control. The first is "Get over yourself. This is about God, not you." This is actually really powerful for me. Without Christ being the central point of the message, I really don't have a lot to share. But when the Scripture and the power of the cross take center stage, I feel a new sense of purpose. It's not about me; it's about Him. And that helps me find courage and purpose.

The second thing I tell myself is "Don't be afraid of these folks. Just love them." Pretty simple, right? But simple does not always mean easy. . . . Loving people who may be judging you, who may be talking about you, who may not like you is hard. But learning to trust God has helped me deal with my fears of judgment and inadequacy as I have shared my faith for decades now. Let me state them again:

1. Get over yourself and just focus on God.
2. Don't fear people; love them.

Do I still get nervous? Yes, pretty much every time. But shifting my focus from myself to God makes all the difference.

What fears do you have when you feel God's prompting to share your faith—whether with one person or a group?

For God has not given us a spirit of fear and timidity, but of power, love, and self-discipline.

(2 Timothy 1:7)

How have you dealt with those fears in the past?

Read 2 Timothy 1:7 in the margin. What does this verse teach us?

For I am not ashamed of this Good News about Christ. It is the power of God at work, saving everyone who believes—the Jew first and also the Gentile.

(Romans 1:16)

Now read Romans 1:16 in the margin. What does this mean for you?

Our Focus Scriptures today explore passages in the Gospel of John that invite people to come and see. In John 1, Jesus invites his disciples to *come and see* where He is staying. Just a few verses later Phillip invites his friend Nathanael to *come and see* the one he believes is the Messiah. And then in John 4, we see the invitation in the story of the woman at the well:

Read John 4:16-18 in the margin. Then reread John 4:25-30 (page 125). Why did the woman invite the townspeople to "come and see" Jesus?

¹⁶"Go and get your husband," Jesus told her.
¹⁷"I don't have a husband," the woman replied.
Jesus said, "You're right! You don't have a husband—¹⁸for you have had five husbands, and you aren't even married to the man you're living with now. You certainly spoke the truth!"

(John 4:16-18)

There is power in the gift of invitation. How have you seen an invitation bless someone in the past? (It could be in a spiritual or non-spiritual setting.)

How does receiving a personal invitation help diminish fear?

After Jesus identifies Himself as the Messiah, the woman goes back into town to urge everyone she meets to *come and see* the man she has just met who knows all about her past.

Come and see is an invitation, and being invited is so much better than not being invited. In college I did some substitute teaching in an elementary school (hats off to the schoolteachers, by the way; it's a challenging role!). On the playground I quickly learned that when the kids got really mad at one another, one of two threats was often used. The first was the "You can't be in our club" threat. The second was the "You're not invited to my birthday party" threat. I spent several afternoons at recess wiping away tears from a kindergartner who was devastated that he or she might not be included.

This fear of not being included is so prevalent today. In fact, society has an acronym for it now: FOMO, Fear of Missing Out. Perhaps that is why it feels so good to be included. It's good to be wanted. I mean, even when we don't really want to be in the club or go to the party, it's nice to be invited, isn't it?

In these scriptural scenarios, Jesus, Philip, and the Samaritan woman are issuing invitations. They simply say, "Come and see," and in response, lives are changed.

Who has been there to encourage you in your faith journey? How did they help you to "come and see" who Jesus is?

Who needs your invitation? (The invitation may be to begin a friendship, come to church, go to Bible study, accept Jesus, go to lunch, or just walk around the block.)

Our heroine this week likely had some fears about sharing Christ in public settings. With her history of having five marriages and now living with another man, there surely had been many who whispered about her. At other times she probably had wished for whispers when she faced open rebuke in the marketplace. But even so, after her encounter with Jesus she is fiercely emboldened to go and share what she has found despite any fears. So she invites everyone she meets to come and see!

There are so many things I have not attempted in life because of fears. Trying out for cheerleading in middle school: fear of failure. Participating in a game show: fear of humiliation. Joining my kids in rock climbing: fear of not being able to keep up. Fears often hold us back from our best life.

What fears might be holding you back from your best life?

Friends, let's be wise, but let's also be fierce and attempt great things for God—despite our fears. Remember the woman at the well, and be encouraged by her example. Whenever you feel His prompting to make a change, share your faith, or to invite someone to faith or friendship, *do it*! Life is short, so let's live it well.

Pray

- Ask God to help you choose to be interruptible in your agenda so that you are ready to respond to the Holy Spirit's promptings.
- Thank God for those who have encouraged your faith.
- Praise God for who He is and for His unfailing love.

DAY 5

Settle

Read and meditate on this verse, rereading it several times in preparation to hear from God today:

[14]How, then, can they call on the one they have not believed in? And how can they believe in the one of whom they have not heard? And how can they hear without someone preaching to them? [15]And how can anyone preach unless they are sent? As it is written: "How beautiful are the feet of those who bring good news!"

(Romans 10:14-15 NIV)

Focus

[18]Then Jesus came to them and said, "All authority in heaven and on earth has been given to me. [19]Therefore, go and make disciples of all nations, baptizing them in the name of the Father and of the Son and of the Holy Spirit, and teaching them to obey everything I have commanded you. And surely I am with you always, to the very end of the age."

(Matthew 28:18-20 NIV)

[21]"Believe me, dear woman, the time has come when you won't worship the Father on a mountain nor in Jerusalem, but in your heart. [22]Your people don't really know the One they worship. We Jews worship out of our experience, for it's from the Jews that salvation is made available. [23-24]From here on, worshiping the Father will not be a matter of the right place but with the right heart. For God is a Spirit, and He longs to have sincere worshipers who worship and adore Him in the realm of the Spirit and in truth."

[25]The woman said, "This is all so confusing, but I do know that the Anointed One is coming—the true Messiah. And when He comes, He will tell us everything we need to know." [26]Jesus said to her, "You don't have to wait any longer, the Anointed One is here speaking with you—I am the One you're looking for."

[27]At that moment the disciples returned and were stunned to see Jesus speaking with the Samaritan woman. Yet none of them dared to ask Him

why or what they were discussing. ²⁸*All at once, the woman dropped her water jar and ran off to her village and told everyone,* ²⁹*"Come and meet a man at the well who told me everything I've ever done."*

(John 4:21-29 TPT)

³⁹*Many of the Samaritans from that town believed in him because of the woman's testimony, "He told me everything I ever did."* ⁴⁰*So when the Samaritans came to him, they urged him to stay with them, and he stayed two days.* ⁴¹*And because of his words many more became believers.*

    ⁴²*They said to the woman, "We no longer believe just because of what you said; now we have heard for ourselves, and we know that this man really is the Savior of the world."*

(John 4:39-42 NIV)

Reflect

We don't know her entire story, but we rarely know anyone's entire story. This woman of Samaria has had five marriages and is now involved with another man. We can pass judgment, and surely many did. But then we wonder, *How did the marriages end*? *Did her husbands die, or was she abandoned*? Either way, we know there has been heartbreak, pain, and perhaps scandal. How has the community treated her? Have they supported her or shunned her through her losses? Are there children? Has she endured times of homelessness and hunger? What burdens, shame, and joy is she carrying as she approaches the well?

Can you see her? Can you imagine her with a downcast face and weary eyes? Surely she must question her worth and purpose. Jesus knows that she comes to the well with a thirst for more than water. She is thirsty for love, belonging, and purpose; and He meets her at this point of need.

In this passage we've seen her ask Jesus some powerful questions that give us clues into her heart and Jesus' compassion. Let's review the first two, which we've explored together previously, and consider the third.

First, she asks, "Why would a Jewish man ask a Samaritan woman for a drink of water?" (John 4:9 TPT). She is shocked that He would speak to her—perhaps that He would notice her at all. She is thirsty for value and love. Jesus speaks to her, and in that speaking He sees her and offers her worth.

Second, she wants to know, "So where do you find this 'living water'?" (John 4:11 TPT). This is a practical question. Tired from all that she has endured in life, she must feel that finding a source of living water—a well that doesn't run dry—would simply make life a little easier. And easy is not what life has been for her.

Third, she asks, "Why do our fathers worship God here on this nearby mountain, but your people teach that Jerusalem is the place where we must worship. Which is right?" (John 4:20 TPT). It's hard to read tone, but I believe this is a sincere question: "Which is right?" In other words, "How can my worship please God?"

You see, the Jews worshiped in Jerusalem at the temple built during King Solomon's reign. The Samaritans, as Jews who had intermarried with foreigners, had built another place of worship at Mount Gerizim during the years that Israel was divided into the Northern and Southern kingdoms. The Jews felt Jerusalem was the only true place to worship since the time of King David. The Samaritans, on the other hand, placed greater importance at Mount Gerizim where they believed Abraham prepared to sacrifice Isaac before there even was a nation of Israel.

So, when she asks which location is right, she is wanting to know how she can please God with her worship—a pure and simple request. Jesus' reply is profound and goes beyond location to matters of the heart.

Reread this passage about what pure worship looks like:

21"*Believe me, dear woman, the time has come when you won't worship the Father on a mountain nor in Jerusalem, but in your heart. . . .* 23-24*From here on, worshiping the Father will not be a matter of the right place but with the right heart. For God is a Spirit, and he longs to have sincere worshipers who worship and adore him in the realm of the Spirit and in truth.*"

(John 4:21, 23-24 TPT)

What does it mean to worship God with the "right heart"?

We continue to have debates over worship today. Perhaps not over location, but what about style? Organ, drums, guitars, hymnals, screens, choirs, robes, jeans—people often have strong opinions about these things.

What styles of worship most appeal to you? Why?

On a mission trip to Central America, my husband, Jim, drove long hours to get to a remote village. In uncharacteristic style he was wearing a clerical collar. When the people of the church saw this, they ran and got saltine crackers and a bottled cola. In very broken English they asked him to consecrate them and serve Communion. Jim struggled for a moment, wondering whether stale saltines and a diet cola could serve for the elements of the Last Supper. But then he looked at their faces. They were hungry to worship. He decided that surely this impromptu unorthodox Communion was pleasing to God.

God is interested in our response to who He is. He longs for us to live our lives as worshipers, not just to attend services of worship. It's not about location or ritual or hymnals, although those things can have meaning. It's about living so that we express our love in pure, sincere, and practical ways. How do we do that? Some beginning steps are spending time with God through prayer and Bible study, treating people with gentleness and patience, going out of our way to do kind acts, and generously sharing whatever resources we with have with our church and those in need.

How would you describe a lifestyle of worship?

What practical steps can you take to move toward this lifestyle?

Taking the message of the cross into the world is the next step of true worshipers. Before Jesus ascends into heaven, He leaves His disciples with marching orders. His last instruction to us is often called the Great Commission.

Reread Matthew 28:18-20 (page 130). What did Jesus commission His disciples, and us, to do?

This commissioning tasks us to go and share Jesus' message and love. Yesterday we saw that the woman Jesus encountered at the well went back to her town of Sychar—and she did so apparently in haste.

Look again at John 4:28 (page 131). What clue do we find in this verse to indicate that she went back to her town in haste?

This woman came to the well to draw water, but she left her water jar behind in order to go invite people to come and see. All at once she dropped her water jar and ran off to her village to tell *everyone*. She took the initiative to go and do the inviting. This is a primary task of followers of Christ.

Now look at verse 39 (page 131). According to this verse, what happened and why?

This is one of my favorite verses, because I want it to be said of me one day too. Many of the Samaritans from that town believed in Him because of the woman's testimony. This woman is not a preacher. She hasn't been to seminary. She simply shared her story, and it impacted many! That's the Great Commission in action. She invited people to come and see, and she took it a step further by sharing her own personal experience.

For years I led a high school girls accountability group. We kept a list of seven covenants and met together weekly to encourage one another to live out our commitments. One of the covenants was to actively seek ways to share our faith in verbal and nonverbal ways daily. During that time, we tried to be sensitive to the Holy Spirit's promptings, and I found myself sharing Christ in situations that never before seemed to have been appropriate. Becoming committed and then being accountable to share how I was living out the Great Commission was life changing for me. I imagine similar opportunities had been there all along and I had just missed them; but when I began to listen for God's promptings, things began to happen.

When have you felt God prompting you to share your faith? How did you respond, and what happened?

How might you become more effective in living out the Great Commission?

Jacob's Well is truly a special place. I hope that if you go to Israel, you'll make the journey into Samaria, now the West Bank, to drink from this water and to imagine the scene where this woman met Jesus. But whether or not we ever visit the actual site of this encounter, we can enter into the story and encounter Jesus for ourselves. And once we encounter Jesus for ourselves, we have the privilege of sharing His love and message with as many people as we can. That's what our fierce woman of Sychar did, and it changed not only her life but also the lives of so many others. She is fierce because she put aside her fears and boldly shared Christ. May the same be said of each of us!

Pray

- Listen to "So Will I" recorded by Hillsong Worship (or another relevant song of your choosing).
- Ask God to lead you to a life of worship in Spirit and Truth.
- Invite the Holy Spirit to lead you to share your faith today with someone in need of Jesus' love.

Video Viewer Guide: Week 4

God often _____ Himself for unique encounters with us.

We, too, need a personal _____ with Christ if we are to live the _____ life promised to us.

"My purpose is to give them a rich and satisfying life." (John 10:10)

When we meet Jesus, whatever the circumstance may be, what will we _____ with Him—how will we _____ to His presence in our life, His commands in His word, and His prodding in our spirits?

"Here I am! I stand at the door and knock. If anyone hears my voice and opens the door, I will come in and eat with that person, and they with me." (Revelation 3:20 NIV)

Week 5

Dorcas

Acts 9

DAY 1

Settle

Listen to "Your Spirit" recorded by Tasha Cobbs Leonard (or another relevant song of your choice) and let it renew, refresh, and energize you for your time with God today.

Focus

³⁶*There was a believer in Joppa named Tabitha (which in Greek is Dorcas). She was always doing kind things for others and helping the poor.* ³⁷*About this time she became ill and died. Her body was washed for burial and laid in an upstairs room.* ³⁸*But the believers had heard that Peter was nearby at Lydda, so they sent two men to beg him, "Please come as soon as possible!"*

³⁹*So Peter returned with them; and as soon as he arrived, they took him to the upstairs room. The room was filled with widows who were weeping and showing him the coats and other clothes Dorcas had made for them.* ⁴⁰*But Peter asked them all to leave the room; then he knelt and prayed. Turning to the body he said, "Get up, Tabitha." And she opened her eyes! When she saw Peter, she sat up!* ⁴¹*He gave her his hand and helped her up. Then he called in the widows and all the believers, and he presented her to them alive.*

⁴²*The news spread through the whole town, and many believed in the Lord.*

(Acts 9.36-42)

Each of you should use whatever gift you have received to serve others, as faithful stewards of God's grace in its various forms.

(1 Peter 4:10 NIV)

Reflect

One of the most precious gifts I have ever received is a tattered quilt. It was tattered when I received it; and after many years of use, it is in barely usable condition. But I love it. It's not particularly pretty. It has varying shades of army green, orange, and purple, with an assortment of brown and red flower patterns thrown in for variety. It was made from scraps and pieced together by hand without the aid of a sewing machine, which resulted in a finished product that is distinctly lopsided. But again, I love it.

Let me tell you how the tattered quilt came to be mine.

When I first married Jim, I worked in an inner-city mission. My daily grind involved ministering to prostitutes, homeless people, drug addicts, and abused children. It was a very tough environment. But through those tumultuous years I made several dear friends. So when it came time for Jim and me to leave for seminary, it was hard to say goodbye to these precious people who had become part of my daily routine.

One particularly hardened older lady of the community that I had come to love was Miss Dilly. When we first met, however, I got the distinct impression that she did not like me. Why did I feel this way? Well, it was because she said something like, "Hey, little blonde girl, I don't like you. You won't last a week here." She wasn't really known for being subtle.

For a while, that's how it was. I worked, and she scowled. If I'm honest, I wasn't really crazy about her either. She talked about me rather nastily behind my back and laughed at me with some of the other ladies of the community. But I was determined to make this ministry work. Day after day I would show up to love on people and counsel with them, and I especially threw myself into developing programs to reach the street children of the community. To the best of my ability, I stayed away from Miss Dilly.

It was about a year later that we had a breakthrough—which involved me losing my cool with her, to which she laughed and said, "Humph, you may just make it after all." A sweet but very unlikely friendship developed.

Together we did what neither of us could have accomplished alone. She had men in the community serve as my protectors when I was outside the center. She let young mothers know that their children would be safe in our programs, and she even encouraged me when things just weren't going well. Then on my last day of work Miss Dilly brought me a gift— the tattered quilt. We were moving from Georgia to Kentucky where she had heard there would be snow, and she wanted to be sure that I would not freeze if I should lose a place to sleep at night just as she had from time to time. So, she had found scraps of material and put together this blanket, my tattered quilt.

The page has blurred as I am writing this, because all these years later I am crying as I remember her loving me in the only way she knew how. The tattered quilt was her way of using the skill she had and the materials at her disposal to show love. And it was precious!

When has someone blessed you through a simple gift?

How does that gift differ from other things you have received?

Who might you bless this week with a simple and meaningful gift?

Miss Dilly's act of love reminds me of Dorcas in the Bible. Like Shiphrah and Puah, we have very little information about the life of Dorcas. The writer of Acts, traditionally thought to be the physician Luke, simply tells us that she was always doing kind things for people, especially those in need.

Reread Acts 9:36-39 (page 139) and Proverbs 20:11 (in the margin). How are our actions, faith, and reputation linked as illustrated in these passages?

Even children are known by the way they act,
whether their conduct is pure, and whether it is right.
(Proverbs 20:11)

Dorcas turned her ability to sew into a ministry and blessed many people. Her acts of kindness were well known throughout the community; and when she passed away, there was such grief that the apostle Peter was summoned in hopes that she might be resurrected.

Reread Acts 9:39. What do the widows do when Peter arrives? What do we learn about Dorcas from this verse?

Dorcas is counted among the heroines of Scripture because through her quiet example we see how we can use our abilities to bless others.

Now, sewing is not a spiritual gift listed in the New Testament. It is an ability, such as baking, babysitting, driving, painting, or writing a note or card. Our abilities may not seem to rate highly when compared to spiritual gifts such as healing and prophecy; but when we use our abilities to bless others, God is honored.

Reread 1 Peter 4:10 (page 139). What are we instructed to do with our gifts and abilities?

What abilities has God given *you* that you could use to bless others? List at least five:

1.

2.

3.

4.

5.

How can you put at least one of these abilities into action by serving others this week?

What steps will you need to take to put this ability into action?

As a teenager, one of my friends was injured and lost the use of his legs. As part of his recovery, the physical therapist made him list all of the abilities he had lost. Running, walking, jumping, skipping, standing, hopping—his list continued, but it was not as lengthy as you may think. She then had him list all of the abilities he had not lost: writing, throwing, reading, reasoning, loving, learning, speaking, teaching, coaching, caring, singing, teaching, laughing—this list went on and on.

What a tremendous exercise in perspective this was. He had indeed lost some abilities. His injuries were extensive, and to this day he is not able to walk. However, he has not allowed his limitations to define him. By using the talents and abilities at his disposal, he has led a full and meaningful life. Instead of focusing on what he lost and what he was not able to do, he chose to use what he did have to its fullest.

There may be times when you feel you have little to offer. I hope in those moments you will remember Miss Dilly and Dorcas. These two women took the abilities and resources at their disposal and intentionally blessed others. As you claim and discover the many talents and abilities God has given you this week, let them be an inspiration for you to serve God and others.

Pray

- Thank God for the abilities and talents He has given you.
- Admit to God times when you felt you had nothing to offer, and prayerfully consider how you can use what you do have to bless others.
- Ask God to show you how He wants to use you today.

DAY 2

Settle

Today let's get creative! If you like to draw, spend a few minutes sketching as God guides you. If you enjoy singing, sing to the Lord. Are you a poet or writer? If so, write God a note today. Express your love to your Creator creatively. He's the master of imagination, and no doubt He enjoys when we connect with Him through our creativity.

Focus

There was a believer in Joppa named Tabitha (which in Greek is Dorcas). She was always doing kind things for others and helping the poor.

(Acts 9:36)

Keep busy always in your work for the Lord, since you know that nothing you do in the Lord's service is ever useless.

(1 Corinthians 15:58b GNT)

God . . . has made us what we are and given us new lives from Christ Jesus; and long ages ago he planned that we should spend these lives in helping others.

(Ephesians 2:10 TLB)

God is not unjust; he will not forget your work and the love you have shown him as you have helped his people and continue to help them.

(Hebrews 6:10 NIV)

Reflect

One of my first opportunities to really serve anyone in ministry came when I was in high school. With skilled supervision, my youth group took on a summer project to replace the roof on the home of an older woman who lived near our church. It was July in Georgia, which means it was really, really hot! The first day of the project was exciting. I bought new work gloves, climbed the ladder, and began removing sixty-year-old asbestos shingles with a passion. Three hours later I had blisters, felt a little cranky, was covered in sweat, and needed a break. We asked the homeowner if we could refill our water bottles from her garden hose, and to our surprise she said no. She didn't want us drinking her water, using her restroom, or playing music in her yard. That didn't sit well with us, but maybe she had her reasons. So, we let it pass without comment.

The next day when we knocked off at 4:00 p.m. from heat exhaustion, she yelled at us for being lazy. Now I was getting aggravated. In fact, it really ticked me off. When I said something to our youth leader, he replied, "The thing about serving others is that sometimes you get treated like a servant." OK, that was a zinger!

That phrase stuck with me. I guess I wanted gratitude—not necessarily applause, but a little appreciation. What I learned that day was that serving others sometimes means being treated as a servant.

Whether there is appreciation or not, we are called to care for the needs of others. Dorcas did this well. In fact, as we read her story in Acts, this is the first thing we learn about her.

Reread Acts 9:36 (page 144). What does this verse tell us that Dorcas did, and how often did she do it?

Dorcas had a reputation in the community as someone who not only observed but also responded to the needs of those around her in practical ways. Most likely there were those who didn't appreciate what she did at times, but apparently Dorcas was not deterred. She just kept right on serving.

Reread Ephesians 2:10 (page 144). According to this verse, how has God planned that we should spend our lives?

Look up Philippians 2:4; Galatians 6:2; and Romans 12:10. What do these verses have in common?

Throughout Scripture we read that we are to do life with one another. We are to care for one another, love one another, help one another, and encourage one another. The list goes on and on. God means for us to live in community. As we do this, we're to be sensitive to the needs of those around us.

How have you spent time helping others recently?

What issues do you see in your community that need to be addressed?

Over the years, one of the issues that has been a constant missional concern in my husband's ministry has been access to clean drinking water in other countries. He has a passion for helping communities dig wells and then plant churches near those life-giving sources of water. As we look back on his ministry, we see that clean water and church planting are a mark of the legacy of his life.

Now, I think clean water is awesome, and I'm all for it; but it's not what makes my heart beat fast. When he gets excited and starts telling me about the next project, I'm supportive and ready to see it happen; but it's not necessarily my thing. For me, my heart has always been about partnering with children in need. Orphaned, abused, enslaved, impoverished—the specifics vary, but God apparently designed my heart with a passion to seek out opportunities to partner with little ones. As Jim sets up churches and digs wells, I want to know how to invest in the next generation—how to help them receive an education, hear about Jesus, and be protected from all the nastiness in the world.

But with so many children in crisis on this planet, it sometimes feels that whatever little thing I can do just doesn't really matter. You may have felt this way before too, wondering, *Can what I do possibly make a difference?*

Over the years I have tried to use whatever influence I have to help others partner with trustworthy organizations that assist at-risk children. So when Compassion International approached us about sharing their work with our congregation, I thought, OK, *great; maybe we can help*. We shared the vision, and I secretly hoped that at least 100 kids would be sponsored—maybe even 150 if we did it well.

Recently I received an email from the vice president of Compassion International letting us know that our local church now sponsors close to one thousand children! Now in the big picture that is still a very small fraction of the hurting children in the world; but it encouraged me. A few days after that we received pictures from a friend in Africa of water pouring from a newly dug well. It was a sweet reminder that God has designed each of us uniquely; and as we use the gifts, abilities, and passions He has given us to help others, the world becomes a little bit better place to live.

What national or global concerns tug at your heart?

What might you do to make a difference in these areas? For starters, consider what organizations already are working in these areas and how you might partner with them.

Reread 1 Corinthians 15:58b and Hebrews 6:10 (page 144). What conditions and promises do we find in these verses for serving others?

Dorcas doesn't get a lot of attention in Scripture. But to those she blessed, she was precious; her work was not useless or wasted. As we saw yesterday, Acts 9:39 tells us that the room in which her body was laid was filled with widows—women who would have been in need—who were grieving the loss of their generous friend. James 1:27 reads, "Pure and genuine religion in the sight of God the Father means caring for orphans and widows in their distress." Dorcas exemplified this verse. Her life was one dedicated to serving the Lord through serving others.

One of the things we say often around our church is "Saved People, Serve People." Caring for others is a natural response to what we have received in Christ. As you reflect on what God has done for you, let Him speak to you about how He would have you to serve others.

Pray

- Take a deep breath and focus your thoughts on God.
- Thank God for choosing to save you and to use you.
- Focus on how your heavenly Father may be wanting to use you to bless others through the passions He has planted in your heart.

DAY 3

Settle

Set a timer for five minutes. You may even want to download an app to help you de-stress and just be still (check out the apps "Calm" and "Abide"). Just be silent and focus on the presence of your heavenly Father, and let Him fill you.

Focus

¹³Now when Jesus came into the district of Caesarea Philippi, he asked his disciples, "Who do people say that the Son of Man is?" ¹⁴And they said, "Some say John the Baptist, others say Elijah, and others Jeremiah or one of the prophets." ¹⁵He said to them, "But who do you say that I am?" ¹⁶Simon Peter replied, "You are the Christ, the Son of the living God." ¹⁷And Jesus answered him, "Blessed are you, Simon Bar-Jonah! For flesh and blood has not revealed this to you, but my Father who is in heaven. ¹⁸And I tell you, you are Peter, and on this rock I will build my church, and the gates of hell shall not prevail against it. ¹⁹I will give you the keys of the kingdom of heaven, and whatever you bind on earth shall be bound in heaven, and whatever you loose on earth shall be loosed in heaven." ²⁰Then he strictly charged the disciples to tell no one that he was the Christ.

(Matthew 16:13-20 ESV)

Jesus looked at him and said, "You are Simon the son of John. You shall be called Cephas" (which means Peter).

(John 1:42 ESV)

There was a believer in Joppa named Tabitha (which in Greek is Dorcas). She was always doing kind things for others and helping the poor.

(Acts 9:36)

Reflect

Do you know what the meaning of your name is? A quick Google search tells me that Jennifer means "the fair one." I do happen to be blond and fair-skinned, but I've known other Jennifers who aren't. Obviously, the meaning of a name does not dictate the attributes or character of the one who holds it, yet in Scripture we do see a lot of meaning associated with names.

For example, we see that Jacob, which means "supplanter," stole his brother's birthright as firstborn. Joshua, which means "Jehovah is his help," led the people, with God's help, into the promised land. Achan, which means "trouble," was stoned for stealing.

We also see in Scripture that names are often changed after people have a significant encounter with God. For some who grew in faith through close fellowship with their Creator, not only did their lives change but also their very names changed to reflect an inward transformation. Today we're going to explore some of these name changes, as well as the bigger picture of what it means to have a good name, saving our heroine Dorcas for the end of our lesson.

Let's begin by looking at a few name changes in Scripture.

Scripture	Original Name	New Name	Details/Insights Surrounding the Change
Genesis 17	Abram		
	Sarai		
Genesis 32:22-28	Jacob		

Though the texts do not always provide the meanings for each name, with a little digging we discover that Sarai, which means "my princess," becomes Sarah, which means "princess of the multitude"; Abram, which means "high father," becomes Abraham, which means "father of many";

and Jacob, which means "supplanter," becomes Israel, which means "one who prevails with God."

One of my favorite name changes in Scripture happens to Jesus' disciple Simon, the brother of Andrew. In Hebrew the name Simon is a derivative of Simeon, which means "God has heard." That's not bad; I like that. But when the disciple Simon has his great encounter with Jesus at Caesarea Philippi, he is given a new name with an even more significant meaning.

Reread Matthew 16:15-16 (page 149). What question did Jesus ask His disciples?

What answer did Simon give?

How did Jesus respond?

While the other disciples report what they have heard—that Jesus is John the Baptist, Elijah, Jeremiah, or one of the prophets—only Simon says, "You are the Messiah, the Son of the living God" (v. 16). This answer pleases Jesus, who responds by changing Simon's name to Peter, or *Petra* in Greek, which means "rock." Simon's name change is an outward symbol of an internal transformation that comes with his faith in Jesus as the Son of God. It also represents a promise of God.

Reread Matthew 16:17-18 (page 149). What does Jesus tell Peter He will do?

When we meet Jesus, our names may not change, but what our names stand for surely should. As others observe your life as a follower of Christ, let them see integrity. Let them observe the fruit of the Spirit—love, joy, peace, patience, kindness, goodness, gentleness, faithfulness, and self-control. Remember that what a name really means comes not from its linguistic origin but from the character of the person who holds it.

Write your first name here: _____

When others hear your name, what qualities do you want to come to mind? Be specific and list five here:

1.

Even children are known by the way they act,
*   whether their conduct is pure, and whether it is right.*
*   (Proverbs 20:11)*

2.

3.

4.

5.

A good name is to be chosen rather than great riches,
*   and favor is better than silver or gold.*
*   (Proverbs 22:1 ESV)*

Now read the Scriptures in the margin.

What does it mean to have a good name?

Faith without works is dead.
*   (James 2:20 NKJV)*

Based on the truths of these verses, what are we to do if we want to have a good name?

Years ago someone came to me complaining about one of my coworkers. I listened to the story and then said, "You know, that makes no sense to me. There must be a misunderstanding, because what you are describing and the person I know simply do not go together." The character, work ethic, and attitude that I had observed in my coworker over many years led me to believe that the story I heard was either a mistake or simply untrue. Through behavior and actions my coworker had established a name that stood for integrity, and hearing otherwise just did not ring true.

Proverbs 20:11 tells us that even children are known by the way they act, by whether their conduct is pure and right. And in Proverbs 22:1 we read that a good name, or reputation, is to be *chosen* rather than great riches. No matter what your name stands for right now, the great news is that you get to choose what it stands for in the future.

Now, what about our heroine Dorcas? Interestingly, her name means "gazelle." Was she swift and graceful like a gazelle? There's no way to know. But what we do know from the few verses in Scripture about her is that it appears she led a simple life filled with kindness and goodness. Her reputation is one that has lasted through the ages as a woman who cared for the poor and was always doing kind things for others. What a great reputation to have. Perhaps she is not fierce in the way we would think of an athlete or an executive, but she is fierce in how she loved the people around her in practical ways.

We are known by our actions, so live in such a way that your actions speak of a life centered in Christ—that when others hear your name, they think of holiness and godliness.

Pray

- Pray the following prayer, or craft your own prayer asking God to help you live a life of kindness and service that brings Him honor and glory:

Lord, help me to live in ways that honor You and bless others. When others hear my name, may it bring to mind traits of integrity and acts of generosity, kindness, and service. Help me to be compassionate, putting my faith into action on a daily basis. Thank You, Lord, for who You are. Today I invite You to shine through me in new and powerful ways. Amen.

DAY 4

Settle

Pray through the Lord's Prayer phrase by phrase, thinking about what each one means for your life:

Our Father, who art in heaven,
>hallowed be thy name.
>thy kingdom come,
>thy will be done on earth as it is in heaven.

Give us this day our daily bread;
and forgive us our trespasses
>as we forgive those who trespass against us.

And lead us not into temptation,
>but deliver us from evil,

for thine is the kingdom, and the power, and the glory
>forever. Amen.[1]

Focus

[25]And a woman was there who had been subject to bleeding for twelve years. [26]She had suffered a great deal under the care of many doctors and had spent all she had, yet instead of getting better she grew worse. [27]When she heard about Jesus, she came up behind him in the crowd and touched his cloak, [28]because she thought, "If I just touch his clothes, I will be healed." [29]Immediately her bleeding stopped and she felt in her body that she was freed from her suffering.

[30]At once Jesus realized that power had gone out from him. He turned around in the crowd and asked, "Who touched my clothes?"

[31]"You see the people crowding against you," his disciples answered, "and yet you can ask, 'Who touched me?'"

[32]But Jesus kept looking around to see who had done it. [33]Then the woman, knowing what had happened to her, came and fell at his feet and,

trembling with fear, told him the whole truth. ³⁴He said to her, "Daughter, your faith has healed you. Go in peace and be freed from your suffering."

(Mark 5:25-34 NIV)

³²Meanwhile, Peter traveled from place to place, and he came down to visit the believers in the town of Lydda. ³³There he met a man named Aeneas, who had been paralyzed and bedridden for eight years. ³⁴Peter said to him, "Aeneas, Jesus Christ heals you! Get up, and roll up your sleeping mat!" And he was healed instantly. ³⁵Then the whole population of Lydda and Sharon saw Aeneas walking around, and they turned to the Lord.

³⁶There was a believer in Joppa named Tabitha (which in Greek is Dorcas). She was always doing kind things for others and helping the poor. ³⁷About this time she became ill and died. Her body was washed for burial and laid in an upstairs room. ³⁸But the believers had heard that Peter was nearby at Lydda, so they sent two men to beg him, "Please come as soon as possible!"

³⁹So Peter returned with them; and as soon as he arrived, they took him to the upstairs room. The room was filled with widows who were weeping and showing him the coats and other clothes Dorcas had made for them. ⁴⁰But Peter asked them all to leave the room; then he knelt and prayed. Turning to the body he said, "Get up, Tabitha." And she opened her eyes! When she saw Peter, she sat up!

(Acts 9:32-40)

Reflect

While in seminary, Jim and I had the opportunity to host an African pastor in our home for dinner a few times. His faith was inspirational, and we loved to hear stories of how God was moving among the people living in the remote villages he served. As he recounted the miracles he had seen, it made us almost jealous to be a witness to that type of movement of God. So I asked him, "Why do you think we don't see these types of miracles in North America with regularity like you do?" He thought for a moment and said, "Every week in the services here the people stand and recite the Lord's Prayer. My people pray this prayer daily too, but when we say, 'Give us this day our daily bread,' it is spoken from the mouths of mothers who hear the rumbles of their children's stomachs as they lay in their beds. They see the distended bellies of their children and know that starvation is slowly killing them. When we pray, we do so out of our desperation to see God move. I don't see that same passion here. Perhaps out of your abundance you have become distant from the One who provides so richly?"

Yes, my friend. Perhaps so.

As we search the Scriptures, we see that most miracles come at a time of desperation. Someone is hurting. People are in need. Human resources have failed. At that point of desperation, God's power shines.

Consider the woman with the issue of blood that we read about in Mark 5. I love this little lady—she is fierce! For twelve years she has struggled medically with a bleeding disorder. The illness most likely left her fatigued and anemic. Although she had seen many doctors, none of them helped her. So in addition to her physical discomfort and pain, she had exhausted her money and her emotions. In fact, the greatest pain she experienced might have come from the emotional and relational trauma of such a condition.

Read Leviticus 15:25-30. What was a woman with an irregular discharge of blood considered to be?

According to Jewish law, this bleeding woman would have been declared unclean and prohibited from being around others. All these years this woman has not been to worship. She has missed celebrations and fellowship. When the ladies of her village gather, she is not invited. She has sought the help of the doctors, and they've brought her no relief. For twelve years she has been isolated, leaving her to suffer physically, emotionally, and even spiritually. But when she hears that Jesus—the rabbi who has done amazing things in nearby villages—has come to her area, she does something daring.

Reread Mark 5:25-34 (pages 154–55). Then read these verses in several other translations, including a paraphrase such as *The Message* **if possible. Look for new insights as you read.**

Consider all that this woman must be feeling as she breaks religious protocol and ventures into the crowd to approach Jesus. Record your thoughts here:

This woman is desperate for a miracle. Physically, emotionally, spiritually, and relationally, she needs restoration. Her only focus becomes Jesus.

In what times of your life have you been able to relate to this woman? When have you been desperate to reach Jesus?

Right before we meet this fierce lady in Mark 5, we read that Jesus has cast a legion of demonic spirits from a man. Jesus is sent away from that area and travels by boat across the Sea of Galilee, where word of His miracles has already reached the distant shore. A large crowd has gathered to see what will happen next. As I picture this scene, I think about a rock concert or political rally. People are pressing in for just a glimpse of the one they've come to see. There is chaos. It is loud, and people are being shoved around in the crowd; but this little lady doesn't care. She is desperate to reach out, to be vulnerable, to receive what no doctor has been able to give her: a miracle.

Then she does what she has come to do. She reaches out—perhaps her first human contact in a very long time. And at the touch of just the hem of Jesus' garment, there is healing.

Look again at verse 29 (page 154). How quickly does the healing take place?

Immediately the bleeding stops, and she can feel that she has been healed.

Again, consider the crowd. Surely there are others pressing in to touch Jesus, and surely some of them have physical issues also. But it is this woman who is healed. Why her? Perhaps because she is the one reaching out with passion and desperation—the kind that the mothers of Africa have when they pray the Lord's Prayer. When we turn to Jesus with our whole hearts, depending on Him and trusting Him to meet our deepest needs, amazing things begin to happen.

Now, let's return to our story of Dorcas. In Acts 9 we see that Peter has traveled from Jerusalem to Lydda.

Reread Acts 9:32-35 (page 155). What is the first thing Peter does in Lydda?

We're told that upon arriving in Lydda, Peter heals a man named Aeneas, who has been paralyzed and bedridden for eight years. When the believers in the nearby coastal city of Joppa (see map on page 159) hear of the miracle, knowing that Peter is nearby, they act quickly.

Now reread Acts 9:36-38 (page 155). What is the request of the believers from Joppa?

Do you think they gave the reason for their urgency? Why or why not?

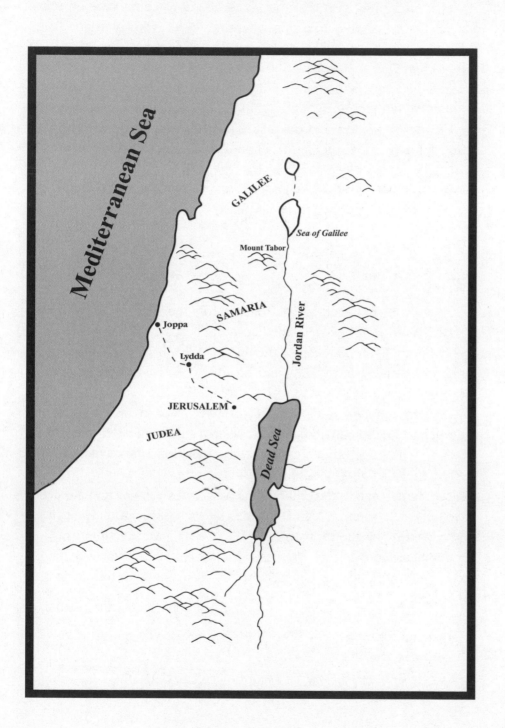

The text simply says that they urged Peter to come without delay, but it's likely that they told him why. Urging Peter to come and bring their dear friend Dorcas back to life is no small request. Verse 37 clearly tells us that Dorcas has died. She is not just sick and in need of prayer. They washed her body to prepare it for burial. But her friends have the boldness of faith to reach out to Peter and ask for a grand miracle.

I love the passion and desperation within their request. And this request, made in love and faith, is honored!

According to Acts 9:39-40 (page 155), what did Peter do when he arrived, and what happened next?

After Peter sent everyone out of the room, he knelt and prayed over Dorcas. Then he told her to get up, and she opened her eyes. Wow! The believers in Joppa received the miracle for which they longed! How amazing that must have been, and how the church in Joppa must have grown as a result of this. (More about that tomorrow.)

Desperation heightens our prayer life. When a friend or family member gets the dreaded diagnosis, when a child we love is in crisis, or when a marriage or other significant relationship is in trouble, we turn to God. And it's right that we do. But all too often we cry out to God only after we have come to the end of ourselves. When science and medicine have failed us, when we're at the end of our resources, when we can no longer control the situation, we cry out to God. I have been guilty of this, and I imagine you have been too. As I look back over my life, I see that in those moments when I get to the end of myself, I am able to fully realize the majesty of God.

Look up John 14:12-14. What is the premise and promise contained here?

When and where have you seen God miraculously show up in your life in the past?

Who needs you to intercede for them right now, praying for a miracle? How can you bless them in real ways today?

I often pray and invite God to do miracles—signs and wonders—in me, through me, and around me. I want my life to be surrounded with the touch of God. I want to see Him at work healing sickness, mending broken relationships, and providing resources in places where there seems to be no hope. It is my joy just to be a bystander and watch God do what only He can. But as my African pastor friend noted, in this country we don't tend to see this as often as believers in other places on the planet do. With advanced medical technology and vast resources, it is easy to become self-reliant instead of God-dependent. Friends, let's not let that be our story.

Rather than wait until we reach desperate times to reach out for the hem of Jesus' robe, let us develop a passion like the mothers of Africa in seeking God's provision, will, and way in our daily lives. Let us be bold like Dorcas's friends in asking God to show up in desperate situations. Remember, God does not always answer our prayers in the way or time that we would like, but He does hear us and love us. And that can give us peace as we seek Him. Then, as our prayers are answered in God's time and God's way, let's be sure to give Him all the glory!

Pray

- As you pray today, ask God to reveal areas in which you need to relinquish control to Him. Pray like the mothers of Africa for those close to you, relying on God for their and your deepest needs and thanking Him for those needs that are met daily and regularly.

- Incorporate Ephesians 3:20 in your prayer, believing that God is able to do more than you can ask or imagine:

God can do anything, you know—far more than you could ever imagine or guess or request in your wildest dreams! He does it not by pushing us around but by working within us, his Spirit deeply and gently within us. (Ephesians 3:20 MSG)

DAY 5

Settle

Stand up and take a deep breath in, reaching over your head as you inhale. Then slowly exhale as you lower your arms. Now try it again. Invite the Holy Spirit in with each breath; and as you exhale, release the stresses that would distract you from this time you will spend with your Creator.

Focus

Let the redeemed of the LORD say so.

(Psalm 107:2 NASB)

Some people brought to him a paralyzed man on a mat. Seeing their faith, Jesus said to the paralyzed man, "Be encouraged, my child! Your sins are forgiven."

(Matthew 9:2)

[40]But Peter asked them all to leave the room; then he knelt and prayed. Turning to the body he said, "Get up, Tabitha." And she opened her eyes! When she saw Peter, she sat up! [41]He gave her his hand and helped her up. Then he called in the widows and all the believers, and he presented her to them alive.

[42]The news spread through the whole town, and many believed in the Lord. [43]And Peter stayed a long time in Joppa, living with Simon, a tanner of hides.

(Acts 9:40-43)

Be rich in good works and generous to those in need, always being ready to share with others. By doing this they will be storing up their treasure as a good foundation for the future so that they may experience true life.

(1 Timothy 6:18-19)

Reflect

Throughout this week we have seen how our heroine Dorcas used her skill as a seamstress to bless others. In fact, her name over the ages has become synonymous with serving those in need. Sunday school classes and mission societies bear her name as a tribute to living in a way that blesses others. She is a great example of exemplifying what we read in 1 Timothy 6:18-19, "Be rich in good works and generous to those in need, always being ready to share with others. By doing this they will be storing up their treasure as a good foundation for the future so that they may experience true life."

We know so little of Dorcas's life, but what we do know of her is that she was generous, kind, hardworking, and compassionate. Her Christ-filled life led her to be so deeply loved that the believers sought Peter's assistance to bring her back to life through God's power after her death. Today as we conclude her story, let's take a look at the long-term effects yielded through God's power at work in her life.

Dorcas's ministry of providing clothing for those in need is precious, but it is what happens after her death that is really attention grabbing.

Reread Acts 9:40-43 (page 163). What did the believers of Joppa do after they saw Dorcas alive again?

According to verse 42, what is the result of their response?

After Peter prays over Dorcas, she opens her eyes and sits up. This gets the people of Joppa talking! And as others hear of Dorcas's miraculous resurrection, many come to believe in the Lord. I love that! As people look at Dorcas, they see a living, breathing example of the power of God at work!

The people of Joppa see that this woman—once laid out and prepared for burial—is now full of life, walking through their seaside village and no doubt sharing how the power of Christ saved her. This captures the attention of the community, and lives are changed. Dorcas's experience and example lead them to believe.

I want that to be true in my life too, and I bet you do as well. But how does that happen if we haven't experienced some incredible miracle as she did? Physical resurrection from the dead most likely will not happen for us before Jesus returns. So can we have an impact in our lifetime as Dorcas did? Yes! Because through Christ we experience *spiritual resurrection*, and that is a miracle that, when shared, impacts the lives of many.

When Jim and I first moved to middle Georgia to launch a new church, we prayed that God would penetrate the hearts of people who were far from God. But our prayer didn't end there. After they received Christ as their Savior, we prayed that they would begin to share what the power of God had done in their lives so that others would be drawn to hear the life-giving message of Christ. As people began to experience the love and forgiveness of Christ and then live their lives in new and holy ways, others far from God began to take notice and come to investigate Christ for themselves. Over the past seventeen years, almost four thousand people have made first-time decisions for Christ in our congregation. We give the glory to God and credit a great deal of those conversions to the fact that, like Dorcas, others can see the effects of Christ at work in us.

I often hear people say that they don't speak much about their faith because it is just too private. This is not a healthy attitude for us to have as believers. Our faith is a deeply personal experience, but it's not meant to be private.

Reread Psalm 107:2 (page 163). What does this verse call us to do?

As we find the courage to share our faith, we put into action the salvation that we have received. In short, *faithful people share their faith*.

As Jim and I prepare to bring the weekend message to our congregation, we often try to incorporate a personal testimony. There is something so very powerful in hearing someone share the change that has occurred in his or her life through the power of God. For example, years ago one of our church members, a prominent businessman, shared about his past struggles with cocaine and depression. His testimony was raw and resonated with many. In the coming weeks, dozens of people came forward to seek help for their particular struggles because his courage led them to find their own. His faith encouraged their faith.

What parts of your story might prove encouraging to others?

There are times when we share our faith through our words, but sometimes we are called to do it through our actions. One of my favorite stories of faith is found in Matthew 9, where some friends bring their sick and paralyzed buddy to Jesus to be healed.

Read Matthew 9:1-7. When the man's friends have trouble getting him to Jesus, what do they do?

When they can't get through the crowd, they climb onto the roof, carrying their friend on a mat. Then they vandalize the property by tearing apart the roof in order to lower him before Jesus. These are dedicated friends! Jesus sees their faith and heals the man.

It's important to note that, in this story, it is the faith of the friends that leads to the healing.

How has the faith of your friends helped to lead you to faith or healing in Christ?

Surely if we were able to read the rest of the story, which is not included in Scripture, we would see that their faith not only led to his physical healing but also to his spiritual healing; that their faith led this once-paralyzed man to receive Christ as his Savior. In fact, it's probably a safe bet that this man's entire family, and perhaps many others, came to know and serve Christ by seeing God's power at work in his life.

What friends need you to do something by faith on their behalf as these men did for their paralyzed friend?

How might you bring them to Christ, as these friends did by lowering him to Jesus? (Consider things such as inviting them to church with you, sharing your faith story with them, praying for them, serving them, inviting them to a small group, or fasting for them.)

You have friends who cannot get to Jesus on their own. They may be paralyzed with doubt, fear, guilt, or shame. They may be crippled with resentment over past hurts or carry pain for which they blame God.

As God's girls, we have received the miraculous gift of life through God's Son, Jesus. In the same way that many were drawn to Christ by seeing Dorcas alive, we have the opportunity for others to be drawn to Christ by seeing Him alive in us. Let the redeemed of the Lord say so! And as the old saying goes, let us use words if necessary.

Pray

- Thank God for the gift of your salvation—the undeserved, precious promise of eternal life in Christ.
- Ask God to give you wisdom about when, where, and with whom to share your faith.
- After being resurrected, Dorcas was a walking reminder of the power of God. Ask God to refine you until you are the same.

God is weaving a beautiful _____ of your life using your talents, abilities, spiritual gifts, and experiences.

When you take a _____ you have been given and use it to bless others, you have turned your talent into a _____; and that brings glory to God.

In the hands of God, our _____ can bless people anywhere and everywhere we go.

Each of you should use whatever gift you have received to serve others, as faithful stewards of God's grace in its various forms. If anyone speaks, they should do so as one who speaks the very words of God. If anyone serves, they should do so with the strength God provides, so that in all things God may be praised through Jesus Christ. To him be the glory and the power for ever and ever. Amen. (1 Peter 4:10-11)

Spiritual _____ are to be used to _____ others and _____ up the church.

Romans 12, Ephesians 4, 1 Corinthians 12

Often our most powerful _____ are our _____ experiences.

Week 6

Lois and Eunice

Acts 16 and 2 Timothy 1

DAY 1

Settle

As we begin Week 6, listen to Nichole Nordeman's recording of "Legacy," if possible. Let the words guide you as you focus on how to unapologetically leave your own legacy of faith.

Focus

¹Paul came to Derbe and then to Lystra, where a disciple named Timothy lived, whose mother was Jewish and a believer but whose father was a Greek. ²The believers at Lystra and Iconium spoke well of him. ³Paul wanted to take him along on the journey, so he circumcised him because of the Jews who lived in that area, for they all knew that his father was a Greek.

(Acts 16:1-3 NIV)

¹Paul, an apostle of Christ Jesus by the will of God, in keeping with the promise of life that is in Christ Jesus,

²To Timothy, my dear son:

Grace, mercy and peace from God the Father and Christ Jesus our Lord.

³I thank God, whom I serve, as my ancestors did, with a clear conscience, as night and day I constantly remember you in my prayers. ⁴Recalling your tears, I long to see you, so that I may be filled with joy. ⁵I am reminded of your sincere faith, which first lived in your grandmother Lois and in your mother Eunice and, I am persuaded, now lives in you also.

(2 Timothy 1:1-5 NIV)

¹⁴But as for you, continue in what you have learned and have become convinced of, because you know those from whom you learned it, ¹⁵and how from infancy you have known the Holy Scriptures, which are able to make you wise for salvation through faith in Christ Jesus. ¹⁶All Scripture is God-breathed and is useful for teaching, rebuking, correcting and training in righteousness, ¹⁷so that the servant of God may be thoroughly equipped for every good work.

(2 Timothy 3:14-17 NIV)

Reflect

What comes to mind when you hear the term "hand-me-downs"? It may create a negative impression for you if you've ever been on the receiving end of some torn-up jeans, old shoes, or a used prom dress. Instead of feeling excited upon receiving these types of gifts, you may have felt disappointment.

But hand-me-downs can also be pretty terrific. When Jim and I got married, we were young, in love, and broke. We were two kids just getting started who were grateful for whatever people were willing to part with, especially furniture. We took a couch from here, a chair from there, a borrowed bed frame, and even my grandmother's thirty-year-old mattress. What's more, we were thankful for it!

Another type of hand-me-down comes in the form of genetics, those traits that we pass on physically—such as height, eye and skin coloring, and predispositions to things like diabetes, cancer, or even addictions.

But the most important hand-me-downs come in a very different form. They are the values, beliefs, habits, and morals that we pass along from one person to the next. Most often they are passed from a parent or grandparent to a younger family member, but they also can be transferred among coworkers, friends, and neighbors. Whether we realize it or not, we are always passing things along. Attitudes, habits, and values are constantly being taught, and through that process we leave a legacy to those who have known us.

What is a habit, trait, or physical characteristic that was passed down to you that you could have done without?

What is a habit, trait, or physical characteristic that you are thankful was passed down to you?

We all have a heritage. We all also have a legacy. But those are very different things. Your heritage is where you come from and what has been passed along to you. Your legacy is what you will pass on to others. Now, you can't do anything about your heritage, but it is completely your choice as to what kind of legacy you will pass on to those who know you, especially those within your tightest circles.

Perhaps you grew up in a healthy situation where you learned good ways to deal with stress, how to disagree without being disagreeable, the benefits of a strong work ethic, and values of honesty and integrity. But not everyone has that. For some people, what was passed along focused more on manipulation, selfishness, and a cynical outlook on life.

The same thing is true for our outlook on faith.

What is your faith heritage? What views were passed on to you regarding God, Jesus, and the church?

How we perceive God, Christ, the church, and God's plan for our life is definitely shaped by how we experienced faith as a child. We can't undo our childhood experiences, though we can and should replace any false and harmful views with the truth. And we can be very intentional about what we are passing on to those around us, especially in this most important area of faith and values.

Some of my earliest memories from my childhood are of church. If I'm honest, part of what I remember about church is painful, having to do with wearing slips and stockings (I hated them!). But on the positive side, once I got over the fancy clothes, I loved being there. The reason for this was mainly a little lady named Mrs. Andrews. She was the lady who greeted me and loved on me every Sunday in the nursery. I remember that she sat in a big rocking chair and that her lap was cushy. She was kind, and her love helped shape my understanding not only of church but also of God's love.

Another treasure of my childhood is that I grew up in a family where faith was an integral part of how we did daily life. My parents modeled Bible study, prayer, and tithing for us. We had family devotions and were held to a strict standard when it came to things such as telling the truth and integrity. My parents were intentional about sharing Christ, and that intentionality paid off for me and my brothers in many ways.

As I reflect on my heritage of faith, it reminds me of the story of Eunice and Lois in the New Testament. They were the mother and grandmother of a young man you may have heard of named Timothy. Timothy's dad was a Greek (Acts 16:3) and, therefore, probably not a believer. But his mother and grandmother, Eunice and Lois, were Jews, and they had come to know and love Christ as their Savior.

Reread 2 Timothy 3:14-17 (page 171). According to these verses, what did Eunice and Lois teach Timothy?

These women were intentional in passing along to Timothy a rich heritage of faith. They knew the importance of teaching young Timothy the Holy Scriptures, which they did from his infancy.

Reread 2 Timothy 3:14-17. Who has shaped your faith story or heritage the way that Lois and Eunice shaped Timothy's (regardless of your age)?

What is one aspect of your faith story or heritage that you hope to pass on?

What is one aspect of your faith story that you do not want to pass on? How will you break that cycle?

When others speak of your legacy, what do you want to be said?

Acts 16 gives us some of the backstory behind the relationship between Paul and Timothy.

Look back at Acts 16:1-3 (page 171). What does Paul hear about Timothy? What happens next, likely as a result of what he has heard?

When Paul went to Lystra to share about Jesus, he heard good things about Timothy's character, so much so that Paul invited him to travel along with him—quite an honor. Timothy became Paul's right-hand man in spreading the message of Christ and helping the first churches work through difficult issues. In fact, he became so important in the work of the church that Paul began six of his New Testament letters by mentioning that Timothy was by his side. He also wrote two very special letters to Timothy, handing down to him instructions about how to lead the churches and how to live faithfully. We know these letters as the books of 1 and 2 Timothy.

Timothy plays a significant role in the New Testament, but we probably never would have known of him if it weren't for two very special ladies who were intentional in helping him develop his faith.

It is beautiful to read in Paul's second letter to Timothy that from infancy Timothy had been engulfed in the love and teachings of Christ.

What a beautiful example to us of how we are to bring up our own children and grandchildren or teach the children God has entrusted to our care or influence.

> **How can you invest in the faith development of others—as Eunice, Lois, and Paul did with Timothy? (Consider opportunities in your family, church, community, or elsewhere.)**

How we share our faith is pivotal in shaping our own lives and the lives of those closest to us. This week as we continue exploring what we can learn from these two lesser-known women of the New Testament, Lois and Eunice, I invite you to focus on your own legacy and how it can enrich the world.

Pray

- Thank God for those who have shaped your life in positive ways for Christ.
- Ask for God's guidance as you intentionally seek to share Him with those around you.
- Examine your habits—good and bad—and ask God to refine you so that your legacy will be one that points to Him in powerful ways.

DAY 2

Settle

Pull out a sketch pad and draw a picture as an offering to God. Don't worry if you're not an artist; just draw a childlike picture. Like a proud mom who rejoices over her child's finger painting, our God rejoices over our sketching (and other creative endeavors) when we do it as a gift to Him.

Focus

Only be careful, and watch yourselves closely so that you do not forget the things your eyes have seen or let them fade from your heart as long as you live. Teach them to your children and to their children after them.

(Deuteronomy 4:9 NIV)

[4]Hear, O Israel: The LORD our God, the LORD is one. [5]Love the LORD your God with all your heart and with all your soul and with all your strength. [6]These commandments that I give you today are to be on your hearts. [7]Impress them on your children. Talk about them when you sit at home and when you walk along the road, when you lie down and when you get up. [8]Tie them as symbols on your hands and bind them on your foreheads. [9]Write them on the doorframes of your houses and on your gates.

(Deuteronomy 6:4-9 NIV)

[36]"Teacher, which is the greatest commandment in the Law?"

[37]Jesus replied: " 'Love the Lord your God with all your heart and with all your soul and with all your mind.' [38]This is the first and greatest commandment. [39]And the second is like it: 'Love your neighbor as yourself.' [40]All the Law and the Prophets hang on these two commandments."

(Matthew 22:36-40 NIV)

Reflect

My grandmother Elizabeth passed away recently at the age of one hundred. In the days following her funeral, I thought about the few trinkets of hers that had been passed on to me: a brooch, a pair of earrings, and a ceramic nest of three little birds. It felt that this was all that remained of her for me. This woman who had been instrumental in my life from the moment I took my first breath was gone. I was surprised that there were so few things left of her. And then it struck me. The real stuff she gave me, the true heirlooms, aren't these trinkets at all. She gave me a rich heritage of love for God and family and a deep commitment to read and study His Word.

I recalled that years ago as I was reading through the Bible cover to cover for the first time, I asked her, "Have you ever read through the Bible?" She replied, "Oh, yes, honey. I think this year will be something like my thirty-fourth time through." I was humbled. Her example of study and steadfastness helped shape my love for God's Word.

Like my grandmother Elizabeth and Timothy's grandmother Lois, I want to be someone who passes on a rich heritage of faith. I'll bet you want to be that kind of woman too. As we talk about leaving a legacy of faith, it's important to remember that, as we've considered previously in our study, values are more caught than taught. We must set an example not only with our words but also with the faithfulness of our behavior.

Talking is easier than doing, isn't it? Telling someone to be patient is so much easier than actually being patient. Talking about gentleness is easier than wrestling a toddler in the grocery store line. But we have to remember that although our words are powerful, our actions are even more impactful.

When our children were small I would often go out on the back deck of our house to pray and study the Bible—and, if I'm being honest, to just have a moment of peace. One hectic day while having deck time, I heard the phone ring, and my six-year-old daughter answered it. Her conversation went something like this: "Hello? . . . Yes, ma'am, she's here. . . . No, I don't think that's a good idea . . . because she's having deck time with God, and that helps Mommy be happy. And today she really needs it. You better call back later."

Wow! Without my using any words, my little girl had picked up on the fact that when I spent time with God, it brought more peace and joy into my life—and evidently made her little life better too. I could have used a lot of words trying to convince her of the importance of quiet time with God, but observing the payoff for herself was much more effective.

That experience reinforced for me the truth that values are more easily caught than taught.

Just like catching a cold or strep throat, we catch what we're exposed to—what those around us are modeling. Timothy caught what Lois and Eunice demonstrated for him. And our kids, coworkers, friends, and neighbors are going to catch a lot of stuff from us. So here's the question we need to ask ourselves: What are the people around us catching? Is it rough language, a temper, a tendency to alter the truth, poor money management, physical aggression, or sarcasm? Hopefully it's much more positive behaviors such as encouragement, faithfulness, kindness, and generosity.

What traits and habits have you caught from others in your life recently?

Who in your sphere of influence may be catching habits from you today? What habits do you want to model for them? Do you have any habits that you would be embarrassed for them to emulate?

Reread Deuteronomy 4:9 and Deuteronomy 6:4-9 (page 177). What do these verses tell us we must do?

Look up Deuteronomy 11:18-19, and put these verses into your own words below:

When asked which of the Old Testament laws was the most important, Jesus responded clearly.

Reread Matthew 22:36-40 (page 177). What did Jesus say are the two greatest commandments?

Jesus said that what is most important is to love God and love other people. He was referring to the passage from Deuteronomy 6:4-9, which instructs us to love God with all our heart, soul, and mind, and then to pass this love of God and God's commands on to our children. This passage in Deuteronomy can be broken down into two sections. The first is what we do for ourselves. We must make God first priority in our lives. We're not going to be able to pass along godly values if we aren't living them. Second, we are to be intentional in sharing God's love and standards, His commands, with those around us. We have to be show-and-tell Christians—showing our faith in our actions and telling about our Savior through our words.

Lois and Eunice must have been show-and-tell women, and Timothy's life reflected their example. Not only was he well versed in understanding Scripture, but he also had outstanding character. The women in his life had been intentional in training him up in the ways of Christ. That training shaped his life—and, in turn, it has shaped the lives of so many others through his example as recorded in the New Testament.

Remember, whether we realize it or not, we are constantly influencing others. Let's live with purpose and intentionally choose language, habits, attitudes, and actions that reflect those of Christ. May we be as intentional as Eunice and Lois were in passing along godliness to those in our realms of influence.

Pray

- Ask God to help you identify those things that distract you from putting Him first in your life.
- Repent of anything that is not a good representation of a Christ follower.
- Commit or recommit to making God's will your first priority.

DAY 3

Settle

Read these verses several times, letting them seep into your heart as you prepare to spend time with God:

"Be still and know that I am God."
> *(Psalm 46:10a)*

I have hidden your word in my heart,
>> *that I might not sin against you.*
>> *(Psalm 119:11)*

Focus

⁴"O Israel, listen: Jehovah is our God, Jehovah alone. ⁵You must love him with all your heart, soul, and might. ⁶And you must think constantly about these commandments I am giving you today. ⁷You must teach them to your children and talk about them when you are at home or out for a walk; at bedtime and the first thing in the morning. ⁸Tie them on your finger, wear them on your forehead, ⁹and write them on the doorposts of your house!"
> *(Deuteronomy 6:4-9 TLB)*

Keep this Book of the Law always on your lips; meditate on it day and night, so that you may be careful to do everything written in it. Then you will be prosperous and successful.
> *(Joshua 1:8 NIV)*

How can a young person stay pure?
>> *By obeying your word.*
>> *(Psalm 119:9)*

I am reminded of your sincere faith, which first lived in your grandmother Lois and in your mother Eunice and, I am persuaded, now lives in you also.
> *(2 Timothy 1:5 NIV)*

14But as for you, continue in what you have learned and have become convinced of, because you know those from whom you learned it, 15and how from infancy you have known the Holy Scriptures, which are able to make you wise for salvation through faith in Christ Jesus. 16All Scripture is God-breathed and is useful for teaching, rebuking, correcting and training in righteousness, 17so that the servant of God may be thoroughly equipped for every good work.

(2 Timothy 3:14-17 NIV)

Reflect

This week as we're considering Lois and Eunice and the influence they had on Timothy, it's natural for us to think about our own influence in the lives of the children we love. After the birth of my first child, a good friend of mine asked me what a win looked like for me as a parent. Honestly, I had never thought about that. In fact, I didn't really even understand her question. She had raised five children who had turned out really well, so I was interested in hearing what she had to say. She continued, "Jen, you've got to know what the wins look like. What do you want this child that God has loaned you to be like at thirty years old? Once you know what that looks like, you can help chisel away everything that doesn't fit that character."

That gave me a lot to think about.

In baseball, a win is determined by how many runners make it around the bases and back to home plate. In business, the win is a positive bottom line on your profit sheet. But what about as a parent? I began to pray and ask God to help me define my parenting win, and then to implement a strategy as a mom that would leave me with as few regrets as possible. A few years later, our son, Josh, was born. As parents, Jim and I had so many goals for our children—health, success, athletics, ministries, academics, careers, marriage—but we quickly realized that all of that was secondary. Our win as parents was for our kids to grow to love and serve Christ. And we really hoped that they also would become our dearest friends as they grew into adulthood.

By defining the win, it put things in perspective. It helped us know what we wanted to emphasize and what things we could let slide. As the old saying goes, we could determine in advance what was a mountain and what was a molehill. For example, a bad grade—that stinks, but we'll get through it. Cut from the starting lineup—that's hard, but it's OK. Lying, not spending time in God's Word, treating people unkindly, disobedience—now that was a different story. Those became "events" in our house. (An event is not a good thing in this case.)

As Alyssa and Josh grew, I would pray over them, "God, please protect these little ones. Make them kind, generous, and obedient to You and us." It wasn't a magic prayer; but if I were to sum it all up, we just wanted them to have loving hearts toward others and especially toward God. More than anything else, we wanted Josh and Aly to know Christ and to follow Him here and for all eternity, ultimately joining us in heaven one day.

Think of your influence in the lives of the children you love (whether or not you are a parent). What have you considered your "win" to be in the past?

What would you like your win to be?

Yesterday we revisited the idea that our values are caught not taught. With that principle in mind, we're going to look in the next few days at habits that are important to model if we want to see those around us grow in godliness. These are things that surely our lesser-known heroines Lois and Eunice modeled for young Timothy. And today we begin with Bible study.

During my years as a youth minister, I would often reflect on Psalm 119:9, which says, "How can a young person stay pure? / By obeying your word." There is both a warning and a promise in this verse. How can young people lead lives that honor God? By living according to the Bible. That's awesome. But if they don't know what's in the Bible, how can they possibly succeed? I became obsessed with helping the students in my little flock learn to personalize and navigate Scripture so that they would know God's standards.

Then I became a mom, and that obsession grew. Even when Aly and Josh were toddlers I began to sing them Scripture songs, and we made games of learning key verses:

Believe in the Lord Jesus and you will be saved.
(Acts 16:31)

Do everything without grumbling or arguing, so that you may become blameless and pure, "children of God."
(Philippians 2:14-16 NIV)

I can do all things through Christ who strengthens me.
(Philippians 4:13 NKJV)

When I am afraid
I put my trust in you.
In God, whose word I praise.
(Psalm 56:3-4a ESV)

These were some of the first sentences they learned. Having worked with so many teens over the years, I knew that my precious little ones would face hard times in life and that their faith would be challenged at times. So, I became proactive in trying to instill in them some core truths on which they could rely.

We considered Deuteronomy 6:4-9 yesterday, but let's take a closer look at these verses:

4"O Israel, listen: Jehovah is our God, Jehovah alone. 5You must love him with all your heart, soul, and might. 6And you must think constantly about these commandments I am giving you today. 7You must teach them to your children and talk about them when you are at home or out for a walk; at bedtime and the first thing in the morning. 8Tie them on your finger, wear them on your forehead, 9and write them on the doorposts of your house!"
(Deuteronomy 6:4-9 TLB)

"Think constantly about these commandments." Perhaps this helps us to understand the verses that follow, which instruct the Israelites to talk about the commandments from morning to night, carry the commandments with them, and even write them on their houses. The Israelites took these verses literally. The men wore phylacteries on their heads, little leather boxes containing Scriptures from the Law or Torah. And every home had a mezuzah, portions of the Hebrew Scriptures written on scrolls inside a decorative case that was affixed to the gates or doorposts of their homes. Even today, Orthodox Jews wear phylacteries, and many Jewish homes have a mezuzah. Why do they do this? These practices are meant to be continual reminders to keep God's Word at the center of all they do.

Not only were they to think constantly about God's commands, but they also were to teach them to their children (v. 7). The New International Version reads, "Impress them on your children." When something is impressed, it literally becomes part of another thing, such as a T-shirt with a graphic impression or someone with a tattoo. Impressing Scripture on others can happen only when we have taken time to impress it into our own lives.

Read and reflect on the Scriptures in the margin. Then respond to the following:

What is the purpose of incorporating Scripture in our lives?

What can you do to impress God's Word deeper into your own life?

Keep this Book of the Law always on your lips; meditate on it day and night, so that you may be careful to do everything written in it. Then you will be prosperous and successful.
(Joshua 1:8 NIV)

Work hard so God can say to you, "Well done." Be a good workman, one who does not need to be ashamed when God examines your work. Know what his Word says and means.
(2 Timothy 2:15 TLB)

All Scripture is God-breathed and is useful for teaching, rebuking, correcting and training in righteousness.
(2 Timothy 3:16 NIV)

What steps can you take to become more intentional in sharing Scripture in your home?

How can you or do you model the importance of Bible study for those in your sphere of influence?

The purpose of studying God's Word is not just to gain knowledge. Knowledge that is unapplied is a dangerous thing because it can produce pride or a false sense of relationship with God. The goal of studying the Bible is life change. As we read in 2 Timothy, the purpose of incorporating Scripture into our lives is so that it may teach us, correct us, and keep us on a straight path that honors God. It also brings blessings into our lives as we live out God's Word.

Now that you know these things, you will be blessed if you do them.

(John 13:17 NIV)

Read John 13:17 in the margin. According to this verse, when are we blessed by knowledge?

This promise doesn't say we will be blessed as we *learn* God's commands but as we *do* them.

Lois and Eunice apparently led Timothy to both know and do the will of God. Paul gives a high commendation of their tutelage in his second letter to Timothy when he writes:

14Continue in what you have learned and have become convinced of, because you know those from whom you learned it, 15and how from infancy you have known the Holy Scriptures, which are able to make you wise for salvation through faith in Christ Jesus. 16All Scripture is God-breathed and is useful for teaching, rebuking, correcting and training in righteousness, [17]*so that the servant of God may be thoroughly equipped for every good work.*

(3:14-17 NIV)

That's what Jim and I wanted to do with our kids. Our win became helping them grow into fully mature disciples of Christ (who enjoyed hanging out with us). We figured if they became devoted followers of Jesus, they might just be spared some of the stuff so many kids fall into, such as cheating, lying, broken relationships, and addictions. It's not foolproof, of course. You can do your best and your kids or the people you invest in can still go astray. But it lays a strong foundation that is more likely to endure.

Are our kids perfect? Nope. Did we get it right all the time? Not even close! But having a defined goal was an important guide for decision-making and discipline.

I hope you will take the time to define your win. If you're not a parent, then what is your win as a person of influence, as a leader, as a follower of Christ? May your win honor Christ in your life and the lives of those around you just as Lois and Eunice did.

Pray

- Seek God's guidance as you define your win.
- Ask God to give you an increased passion to study, understand, and memorize His Word.
- Thank Him that He has already let us know through His Word what is most important in life: to love Him and to love other people!

DAY 4

Settle

Read the first portion of Psalm 103, which is the basis for the song "10,000 Reasons." Then, if possible, listen to this song recorded by Matt Redman.

Focus

[8]*"Should people cheat God? Yet you have cheated me!*

"But you ask, 'What do you mean? When did we ever cheat you?'

"You have cheated me of the tithes and offerings due to me. [9]*You are under a curse, for your whole nation has been cheating me.* [10]*Bring all the tithes into the storehouse so there will be enough food in my Temple. If you do," says the* Lord *of Heaven's Armies, "I will open the windows of heaven for you. I will pour out a blessing so great you won't have enough room to take it in! Try it! Put me to the test!"*

(Malachi 3:8-10)

[14]*But as for you, continue in what you have learned and have become convinced of, because you know those from whom you learned it,* [15]*and how from infancy you have known the Holy Scriptures, which are able to make you wise for salvation through faith in Christ Jesus.* [16]*All Scripture is God-breathed and is useful for teaching, rebuking, correcting and training in righteousness,* [17]*so that the servant of God may be thoroughly equipped for every good work.*

(2 Timothy 3:14-17 NIV)

[24]*And let us consider how to stir up one another to love and good works,* [25]*not neglecting to meet together, as is the habit of some, but encouraging one another, and all the more as you see the Day drawing near.*

(Hebrews 10:24-25 ESV)

Reflect

With Lois and Eunice as our inspiration, yesterday we talked about defining our win as influencers, especially in the lives of the children we love. We also began to dig into some of the habits worth intentionally modeling to those around us. We started with the importance of Bible study and applying what we learn from Scripture in our daily lives. Today we're going to dig into three more important life habits: prayer, tithing, and accountability.

Pray

By simple definition, prayer is communicating with God. Just as in any other relationship, this will involve both talking and listening. Prayer is supernatural, and it is hard for our minds to comprehend how the God of the universe could hear and respond to us. But He does! In fact, in Acts 17:28 (NIV) we learn that "in him we live and move and have our being." He is as near as our breath, and He wants us to talk with Him authentically and intimately—as simply and honestly as we can.

What was prayer like in your home when you were growing up?

How would you describe your prayer life now?

Read these verses on prayer, and consider what they mean for your life and the lives of those you influence. Make notes in the space provided:

Philippians 4:6

John 15:7

Matthew 6:5-15

Developing our own prayer life and helping our children (or those younger than us) develop their own communication with God is fundamental to a healthy faith. A lifestyle of vibrant prayer is such an essential tool in connecting with our Creator and leaning into His love and wisdom.

Tithing

The practice of tithing, which is giving a first tenth of your resources to God, is such a powerful tool in shaping our faith. In the Old Testament God instructs His people to always keep Him first by setting aside the first and best of what they have and giving it as an offering to the Lord. Being in ministry for so many years, I have noticed that people who don't practice this spiritual discipline don't want to talk about it out of conviction, and people who do practice it don't want to talk about it out of humility. So, nobody wants to approach the topic. I get it. We can be funny about talking about our money!

But let me be transparent and tell you what I have seen again and again, and what I have personally experienced. You simply cannot out-give God.

As I've shared previously, Jim and I began our marriage with very little. I worked in a mission, and we actually qualified for groceries out of the food pantry even as we both worked full-time jobs. But during that lean season, we were faithful to tithe. In return, God blessed us. He blessed us spiritually but also financially. We have found that like a good and generous parent, God longs to reward those who are faithfully following Him. He waits for us to line up with His standards so that He can shower us with blessings. But what good parent would reward a disobedient child? That would not be good parenting.

Read Malachi 3:8-10 (page 188). What is the promise in this passage that God gives to those who are faithful with the tithe?

Read Luke 6:38 and Proverbs 3:9-10 in the margin. What do these passages teach us about generosity?

"Give, and you will receive. Your gift will return to you in full—pressed down, shaken together to make room for more, running over, and poured into your lap. The amount you give will determine the amount you get back."

(Luke 6:38)

9Honor the LORD with your wealth
 and with the best part of everything you produce.
10Then he will fill your barns with grain,
 and your vats will overflow with good wine.

(Proverbs 3:9-10)

When I think of spiritual disciplines—things such as Bible study, prayer, tithing, and accountability—tithing is the one I know I can get right. I can be obedient and practice tithing by making it a regular part of my life. I remember watching my parents write the check that they would later put into the plate at church. One-tenth of their income compared to my five-dollar allowance seemed like a fortune. But I was struck with their obedience and how in good times and hard times they honored God first. I encourage you to practice tithing and watch God make good on this promise in your life. Do it even for a season and ask God to reveal Himself to you during that time. The added benefit is that it just may end up blessing generations to come as they follow your example.

What is your experience with tithing? If you do not currently tithe, would you be willing to trust God and try it for a season to see how He may bless you? Why or why not?

Accountability

Allowing other Christ followers into our lives in order to hold us responsible and encourage us as we live out our faith is the practice of accountability. It is possible to grow in Christ on your own, but it is done best in community. Choosing godly friends who will both hold you accountable and encourage you will model to those around you the value of doing life with the family of God. As we seek to walk closely with Jesus, we need to surround ourselves with like-minded women of God who will help us to sharpen our faith.

Walk with the wise and become wise, for a companion of fools suffers harm.
(Proverbs 13:20 NIV)

As iron sharpens iron, so a friend sharpens a friend.
(Proverbs 27:17)

Read the proverbs in the margin. What do these verses mean? Write each below in your own words:

Proverbs 13:20

Proverbs 27:17

I have often quoted Proverbs 13:20 to my children. With these and similar verses in mind, we must choose carefully those we let into our inner circle. We must be wise about who we allow to shape our hearts and minds—and the hearts and minds of our children. And we must be intentional to build these close relationships so that there is a depth of friendship that allows us to speak kindly but freely in order to correct, advise, and encourage. This kind of bond takes time.

Reread Hebrews 10:24-25 (page 188). What does this passage instruct us to do?

How have close Christian relationships shaped your life?

What are your longings or needs right now related to healthy accountability?

Of the four disciplines we have covered yesterday and today—Bible study, prayer, tithing, and accountability—which one is easiest for you? Which one is most difficult?

We can't know fully how Timothy's mother and grandmother prepared him to be a Christ follower. But we do know that when Paul came to Lystra, Timothy's reputation as a faithful young man stood out from the crowd. We also know that Paul gave these two women a great deal of credit for the faith he saw in young Timothy. Teaching him to study the Scriptures, communicate with God through prayer, and live generously and practice the tithe all while living in community with other believers were surely fundamentals of his Christian education. As we seek to live Christlike lives, these are the habits we must model and pass on to the next generation. Let's do it well.

Pray

- Thank God for those who have sharpened you in your Christian life.
- Ask God to give you a heart to desire His Word, long for prayer, and seek to live generously.
- Seek God's direction about how you can wholeheartedly and effectively pass on your faith to others.

DAY 5

Settle

As you prepare to hear from God today, just be still. You may even want to set a timer and give yourself several minutes to just be. No one to talk to, no phone to answer, no emails to return. Just be present and allow God to speak to you in the solitude.

Focus

"But watch out! Be careful never to forget what you yourself have seen. Do not let these memories escape from your mind as long as you live! And be sure to pass them on to your children and grandchildren."

(Deuteronomy 4:9)

22But the Holy Spirit produces this kind of fruit in our lives: love, joy, peace, patience, kindness, goodness, faithfulness, 23gentleness, and self-control. There is no law against these things!

(Galatians 5:22-23)

3I thank God, whom I serve, as my ancestors did, with a clear conscience, as night and day I constantly remember you in my prayers. 4Recalling your tears, I long to see you, so that I may be filled with joy. 5I am reminded of your sincere faith, which first lived in your grandmother Lois and in your mother Eunice and, I am persuaded, now lives in you also.

(2 Timothy 1:3-5 NIV)

In your hearts honor Christ the Lord as holy, always being prepared to make a defense to anyone who asks you for a reason for the hope that is in you; yet do it with gentleness and respect.

(1 Peter 3:15 ESV)

Reflect

One of my favorite things about being a parent is hearing the crazy stories my kids tell me. A few years ago, while Jim was away at a conference, we had a knock on our door at about 9 p.m. That's late for us on a school night, and I was already in pajamas. The knock was persistent, so I went to the door anyway. There stood a fireman in full gear. I figured he was collecting for the volunteer fire department, so I cracked the door and asked him if he could come back at another time. He calmly looked me in the eyes and said, "Well, no, ma'am. There's a fire in your backyard, and we have six trucks on their way over right now." I turned around to see our son, who had just come in from the yard, sort of sink into the couch. Nice—six fire trucks, no husband, and me in my pajamas while a fire blazed in our backyard. Great! I'll come back to this story a little later.

Parenting is an adventure. There are lots of precious moments and many heart-wrenching challenges. Time goes quickly, and if we aren't intentional we may not make the most of every opportunity to instill godly values into the next generation. We may overreact to the trivial and not make a big enough deal about things of eternal consequence.

In our devotional lessons this week we have talked about defining your win. You may have given that additional thought in the past few days. As a mom, grandmother, aunt, teacher, or someone else who has influence over others—and we all do—it's important to define what matters most. What does a win look like? In schools, teachers are given benchmarks that each child is to reach by a certain age. It gives the teacher a guideline of how the student is doing and defines the teacher's win as a classroom leader. We, too, need benchmarks so that we know how we're doing and how those around us are faring.

We've looked at Deuteronomy 4:9 several times this week, and it's fitting that we wrap up our study with a final look at this significant verse, because living out this verse is one of the surest ways to become a fierce woman of God.

Reread Deuteronomy 4:9 (page 194). How does this verse speak to you in your current phase of life?

What additional thoughts do you have about defining your win—as a Christ follower and a person of influence?

For me the win has been to help cultivate fully devoted followers of Christ—both in my home and my other spheres of influence. Perhaps your win is similar. But how do we measure that?

To some degree it may seem to be a subjective goal. But there are mile markers to help us gauge how we're doing on this adventure. I'd like to briefly share five tools I've used that are helpful as we evaluate how we're doing with passing along godly values and skills. We have talked about some of them throughout our study, but this gives us a nice summary:

Navigate the Bible. This is the ability to know and use the Bible for yourself, to be familiar with the content and know how to find passages independently. Some keys to achieving this goal include having a Bible that is easily understandable and age appropriate for the reader; incorporating Bible reading and study into daily life; and being exposed to healthy Bible teachers and resources.

Do your best to present yourself to God as one approved, a worker who does not need to be ashamed and who correctly handles the word of truth.

(2 Timothy 2:15 NIV)

Personalize Scripture. This means bringing a verse to life by making it relevant to your everyday experience. For example, we may read, "For God so loved me that He sent His Son, Jesus, for me" (John 3:16); "While I was still sinning, Christ died for me" (Romans 5:8); and "How do I keep my way pure? / By living according to God's word" (Psalm 119:9). Knowledge without personal application does us no good and, in fact, can lead to a false sense of security or even pride. So, learning to weave Scripture into our personal lives is key. As I read Scripture I constantly ask myself the question "So what?" This is not a sarcastic question but a question we ask for greater depth of application. For instance, "So what does this mean for my life? So what sin should be avoided? So what action needs to be taken? So what does God want me to do with this spiritual truth?" By personalizing His Word, it helps mature and mold us into the women He created us to be.

For the word of God is alive and active. Sharper than any double-edged sword, it penetrates even to dividing soul and spirit, joints and marrow; it judges the thoughts and attitudes of the heart.

(Hebrews 4:12 NIV)

Articulate your faith. This is simply putting into words what God has done and is doing in our lives so that we are ready to live out the Great Commission. By being prepared to share Christ when opportunities arise, our faith is more likely to have a lasting impact on others' lives. Although our faith is a deeply personal experience, it is not meant to be kept private.

Let the redeemed of the Lord tell their story—
those he redeemed from the hand of the foe.

(Psalm 107:2 NIV)

Make wise choices. As we've seen, personalizing Scripture helps us know what Christ has done for us and teaches us how we are to live in ways that please God. But knowing and doing are not always the same! At times, we and those we influence may be educated beyond our level of obedience. In other words, we can have wisdom but not always choose to make wise choices. A good example of that is Solomon, the wisest man who ever lived. Despite his wisdom, Solomon did not always choose wisely. This benchmark moves beyond knowing to doing. It is the step of choosing to live with integrity even when it is inconvenient and countercultural.

Do not forsake wisdom, and she will protect you;
love her, and she will watch over you.

The beginning of wisdom is this: Get wisdom.

Though it cost all you have, get understanding.

(*Proverbs* 4:6-7 NIV)

Display the fruit of the Spirit. According to Galatians 5:22-23, this fruit is love, joy, peace, patience, kindness, goodness, faithfulness, gentleness, and self-control. The degree to which these godly characteristics are evident in our lives is a great benchmark for evaluating our progress. They are the by-products of a heart surrendered to God.

My husband, Jim, often says that you can't really lead anyone down a path you're not traveling yourself. With that in mind, I invite you to assess yourself in these five areas.

With 1 being a beginning point and 5 being a regular practice, rate yourself in each area:

Navigate the Bible	1	2	3	4	5
Personalize Scripture	1	2	3	4	5
Articulate your faith	1	2	3	4	5
Make wise choices	1	2	3	4	5
Display the fruit of the Spirit	1	2	3	4	5

In which of these areas do you feel you excel and are confident?

In which areas do you feel you need to do some intentional work?

What action steps can you take this week?

Now back to the backyard fire. Josh owned up to it quickly, and that drastically changed the outcome of this story for him. He hadn't meant to start a fire, at least not a big one. His repentant heart and quick admission of guilt helped us move on from this incident without it becoming a huge ordeal. It was somewhat embarrassing to me because of the six fire trucks. But it was not an intentional act of defiance on Josh's part, and that helped me to keep it in perspective. We did the safety talk about lighters, and he promised to be safe; but because his integrity was so strong, he avoided significant punishment. The experience was an opportunity to see how our values had "stuck" and also to reinforce the importance of integrity and honesty.

Take a moment to assess someone with whom you have influence:

Navigate the Bible	1	2	3	4	5
Personalize Scripture	1	2	3	4	5
Articulate your faith	1	2	3	4	5
Make wise choices	1	2	3	4	5
Display the fruit of the Spirit	1	2	3	4	5

What are the person's strengths? How can you encourage him or her to continue in that?

In what areas do you need to become intentional about helping this person develop?

How can you help him or her with these goals this week/month/year?

Taking an honest look at these mile markers may give you an indication of how you are spending time guiding your own spiritual life as well as the spiritual lives of those around you. Lois and Eunice, our heroines this week who are helping us wrap up our study, were intentional to raise young Timothy in such a way that he stood out among all of the other men of the community. Their wise instruction is famously commended by Paul in both Acts and 2 Timothy. They are an example of women who intentionally poured Christlike values into their family—and no doubt affected all who came into contact with them. May we do the same!

We have each been given a heritage, but the legacy we leave for others is ours to choose. Let's choose well. Let's learn from each of the fierce women we have studied, facing the challenges of our lives with the courage of Shiphrah and Puah, the midwives of Egypt; the faith of Naaman's slave girl; the wisdom of Deborah; the humility of the woman at the well; the compassion of Dorcas; and the intentionality of Lois and Eunice. Let's be fierce!

Pray

- Pray the following prayer, or craft your own prayer asking for God's help in pouring His love and character into the lives of others:

God, may we, like Timothy's mother and grandmother, be faithful. May we become consumed with sharing Your love and the message of Your Son's gift of salvation. Father, break our hearts for what breaks Yours. Give us wisdom and insight to function in our families and beyond in winning and effective ways that lead those we love to the very foot of the cross. Amen.

- Lift up family members and other loved ones by name and situation to the Lord, asking Him to reveal to you how you can best serve them today.
- Ask God to reveal how *you* are a fierce woman of God and what you can do to become even more fierce for Him.

Video Viewer Guide: Week 6

God calls us back into places of _____ to do tremendous
_____.

Paul came to Derbe and then to Lystra, where a disciple named Timothy lived, whose mother was Jewish and a believer but whose father was a Greek. The believers at Lystra and Iconium spoke well of him. Paul wanted to take him along on the journey. . . . As they traveled from town to town, they delivered the decisions reached by the apostles and elders in Jerusalem for the people to obey. So the churches were strengthened in the faith and grew daily in numbers. (Acts 16:1-5 NIV)

I am reminded of your sincere faith, which first lived in your grandmother Lois and in your mother Eunice and, I am persuaded, now lives in you also. (2 Timothy 1:5 NIV)

We have to _____ the behaviors we want to see the children in our lives emulate.

We have to be sure that we are guiding the children in our lives to become _____ _____ of Christ—generous, kind, and filled with the fruit of the Spirit.

Watch what God does, and then you do it, like children who learn proper behavior from their parents. (Ephesians 5:1 MSG)

Video Viewer Guide Answers

Week 1

control
aware / combat
criticism
faithfulness

Week 2

joy / purpose
ourselves / through
excuses

Week 3

kindness / unkind
sin / loves

Week 4

positions
encounter / full
do / respond

Week 5

tapestry
talent / ministry
abilities
gifts / bless / build
experiences / painful

Week 6

pain / ministry
model
mature disciples

Notes

Week 1: Shiphrah and Puah

1. Robert B. Strimple, "The Fear of the Lord," The Orthodox Presbyterian Church, www.opc.org /new_horizons/NH01/03a.html.
2. Quotations from Irena Sendlerowa, History's Heroes? website, http://historysheroes.e2bn.org /hero/howviewed/4332.
3. Adam Easton, "Holocaust Heroine's Survival Tale," BBC News, March 3, 2005, http://news.bbc .co.uk/2/hi/europe/4314145.stm.
4. "Irena Sendler Biography," The Biography.com website, March 21, 2016, www.biography.com /activist/irena-sendler.
5. Ashton Applewhite, Trip Evans, and Andrew Frothingham, And I Quote, rev. ed. (New York: St. Martin's, 2003), 24.

Week 4: The Samaritan Woman

1. David Black, "The Callings," New York Times Magazine, May 11, 1986, www.nytimes.com/1986/05 /11/magazine/the-callings.html.

Week 5: Dorcas

1. "The Lord's Prayer," The United Methodist Hymnal (Nashville: The United Methodist Publishing House, 1989), 270.